MAKING DOLLAR$ AND SENSE ON WALL STREET

By: D. Scott Goodrick

MAKING DOLLAR$ AND SENSE ON WALL STREET

This book is dedicated to my parents Robert and Billie Goodrick

The entire time I was writing this book I was always thinking, "Why do authors always dedicate their book to their parents?" Now I know. It's because when I look back and read my writing I can see my parents' life lessons they taught me as I was growing up. This book is a reflection of them and I am so happy to have learned that message in the writing process.

Important Information

The Information contained in this book is for educational and illustrative purposes and should not be considered investment advice. The opinions expressed are those of the author, however biased or poor they may be.

This book was written for investing in a utopian community where all investments are available in every 401k or investment account. This clearly isn't the case, so the reader is responsible for adapting the concepts in this book to their current situation.

Investing is a dynamic process. Like farmers and their crops, investments need constant attention to produce an optimal harvest.

By reading this book you will learn the author's basic investment style. This is powerful information and can greatly increase your wealth and comfort level by investing. Like all knowledge, it can be twisted or used to create the opposite effect. Moderation is always the best practice.

Table of Contents

Chapter 1

HOW DID I END UP ON WALL STREET

I'm frequently asked, "Why did you decide to go into investments and finance as a career?" I guess the answer goes back to my childhood memories, a little research, and just plain dumb luck.

One of my earliest life memories was when my father took my two older brothers, my older sister and myself to a bank one evening for some type of presentation about stocks in the 1960's. I was probably six or seven years old. What really stuck in my mind about the evening was that after the presentation we were offered drinks and cookies. I looked over the tray of assorted goodies and picked out the most wonderful-looking cookie in the whole world. It had a glowing red half-circle decoration on top of it. This red decoration on the cookie was brighter than any marble I had ever seen. Something this beautiful had to be the best-tasting thing on the planet.

I picked up this wondrous cookie and ate all the way around the edge until all that was left was the glorious red glowing semicircle and cookie beneath it. I closed my eyes and popped this morsel into my mouth. The taste was nothing like I had ever eaten before. I mean the taste was HORRIBLE! I spit the foul concoction out of my mouth and into the napkin in my hand. I then gulped my drink down to remove the vile taste from my mouth. The word I still use today to describe this nasty red thing is 'YUCKY!' Needless to say, I have never again eaten

1

anything that has any of those red round things on it.

The next and most influential investment memory is the day the Dow Jones Industrial Average broke 1000 for the first time. My father let me stay home from school for the day. I knew that something big was about to happen. We were sitting in the den watching the television; the ticker was streaming across the bottom of the screen. He taught me how to read what all the numbers and symbols meant on the ticker. This was before cable television so I think some national channel must have put the ticker on as a special one-time deal. Anyway, I was there glued to the television most of the day and there it went, the DOW broke 1000. It didn't finish the day over 1000, but I was there to see this event.

I took the long road to college. I had wild adventures and difficult challenges to meet before I eventually got there. I graduated from High School and went into the US Marine Corps, which was the best decision I ever made in my entire life. When I was honorable discharged four years later I then went to work in my parents' party rental business in Cleveland, Ohio. At the age of 26 I had reached the pinnacle of my career in this company. Looking at my upcoming 27th birthday I had my midlife crisis; I knew that there had to be more in life than working this same job until I retired. As I grew up I really didn't think I would live to the age of thirty. Now it looked like I was going to live past that age; I simply hadn't planned this far out! I again needed some direction on what path I wanted to take on the road of life.

I spent a lot of time thinking about what I wanted to do with my life. I was sure there was more to life than what I was looking at. I started to ask retired people I knew one question: "Looking back, what would you have done different with your life?" They all had the same answer: "Play More!" Most of those asked had gone to some war or another after high school or straight to college. They then started a job and a family. The hook that solidified this idea of "Play More!" and really grabbed me was the way one police detective explained the concept to me. You retire at 65. You work 25 years to get a pension, 65-25=40. You don't have to get a real job until you are 40 years old! The one thing that you needed was a four-year college degree before turning 40 to make the math work out properly.

I spent a few months figuring out how I wanted to play, and I wrote a list of things I wanted to do. It didn't matter if I was qualified to do that task or job, this was a 'wish' list and a 'real' list combined. I also wrote a list of the jobs I didn't want to do. I took a month to complete the two lists, and these lists stayed with me constantly for that month. I then threw away the list of jobs I didn't want to do; I would remember most of them.

I started to cross the jobs I knew I couldn't do off the list that I wanted to do. The first was Space Shuttle Astronaut. I had applied for this program in the late seventies but had never heard back from NASA. Fighter pilot went next, my eyes need glasses to see properly, and I was too old. The list was slowly reduced over a week or so to a handful of jobs: Farmer, Park Ranger, Rancher, and Whitewater River Guide. The theme I took from this was that I wanted a job outdoors where I could be physically active.

I did some research on the park ranger position. You had to work for the government and it seemed very political, and not highly praised work. After four years in the Marines I had worked for the government long enough. It was time for a road trip. I visited a few whitewater river outfitters in West Virginia, North Carolina and Tennessee. I then headed west to look at farms and ranches. As I headed west past Indianapolis all I saw were huge agribusinesses. I was looking for a small farm, but I didn't see any of these. I knew they were out there but mile after mile all I saw were machines working the land, no people about at all. I turned my car around; I was going to be a river guide!

I sold everything I couldn't physically carry and headed to West Virginia for the summer of 1987. I spent that winter in Costa Rica as a river guide. The summer of 1988 was spent on the commercially rafted rivers in Tennessee, Georgia, North Carolina and South Carolina. I went to Florida to work construction that winter, but I ended up becoming an ocean lifeguard for the City of Hollywood, Florida. In the spring of 1989 it was back to West Virginia for my last season of being a river guide and the best summer of my life. I worked for North American River Runners (NARR) on the New, Gauley, and Cheat Rivers. NARR is a world-class operation and a leader in the rafting industry. I then made the final transition from whitewater river guide to ocean lifeguard for the city of Hollywood, Florida. I made a deal with the captain of the beach patrol. I would work as a lifeguard until I finished college if he would split my days off so I could attend college full time two days a week; he agreed.

This was during the time when *Baywatch* was high on the ratings. This made my job even more interesting with all the attention I received from the ladies. I did manage to get my bachelor's degree in Finance from Florida International University while working full time as a lifeguard, and in four years. The college loans needed to be repaid so I had to start looking for a real job before my fortieth birthday. When the college loans were paid off, I started racing cars and did that for about six years. My next book is about my wild, dangerous, funny and outlandish adventures I lived through while in the Marines, River Rafting, Lifeguarding and Racing Cars.

I graduated college at the age of 36 with a Bachelor's of

Business Administration in Finance from Florida International University. I had learned through my travels and adventures that more CEO's had finance degrees than any other degree. In the world of business you have to know how money works. I was living in South Florida, which is a long distance away from the physical Wall Street located in lower Manhattan, New York. In my senior year in college I looked in the Yellow Pages for investment houses situated locally in south Florida, but all I could find was the Franklin Templeton headquarters. Well, off went a résumé; I never received a reply back. Off went another résumé without a reply. I applied for a position on of their Internet site but still received no reply. Hmmm, not a good start, I couldn't even get an automated "We received your résumé and will contact you if your skills match the position."

To make a long, boring story short, I was finally hired as a stockbroker with Dean Witter in Hallandale, Florida, and I entered their six-month training program. On my first day of actual work I got an interesting phone call. It was from Sparky, a former Hollywood Beach lifeguard I worked with who had also turned stockbroker for another big investment house. He had heard a rumor that there were rideable surfing waves about a two-hour drive north and asked if I wanted to go surfing. "What? Are you NUTS? This is my first day of work!"

"Calm down," he replied. He then proceeded to explain that as a stockbroker you set your own hours and most work actually occurs after normal business hours. I told him I would have to talk to the branch manager about taking the day off and then get back to him.

I walked over and knocked on the door of the branch manager, Don. This was the man who had hired me. He motioned me in and to sit down while he finished up a telephone call. When the call was over he asked me, "How things are going? Any problems?" The normal dialog that you would expect on someone's first day at work. It is the start of building a foundation of knowledge about the strengths and weaknesses of the people that work for you.

After a few minutes of normal business chat I decide to pop the question. I mentioned that it was pretty windy that day. He acknowledged that statement with a low-pitched growl as he gazed at some paperwork in front of him. I next stated that winds usually brought large waves near the shoreline. This caught his interest and keeping his body rigid, he moved only his eyeballs up so he could peer over his reading glasses and give his full attention to the conversation at hand. "OK," was all that he said, acknowledging my second statement and wondering where this conversation was going.

"Well, I'm a surfer and we don't get rideable waves very often. I guess I'm asking for the rest of the day off to go surfing."

Without a blink he said, "Sure, go ahead, have a good day." I got up and headed back to my office to call Sparky back and make arrangements for the afternoon surfing session.

I was heading for the front door to start another surfing adventure, but just as I was about to grab the doorknob Don called out my name, "Scott!"

I turned around and headed towards his office. I only stuck my head into his office, hiding the rest of my body around the corner. "Scotty." *OH!* He had said my name twice; I made a mental note that this was going to be important. "If you fail the Series 7 test, I will fire you." The sentence came out more as a statement of fact than as a threat. The Series 7 test is required before you can sell stocks, bonds and mutual funds. To pass that test within five months was my first job priority. I responded that the test wouldn't be a problem and off I went.

I passed the Series 7 test a few months later, with highest score ever in the office, along with a couple of other investment series tests that were required to sell investments in all fifty states in addition to some insurance and managed futures products. It was then off the Manhattan and the World Trade Center for a month to learn about the wonderful world of working for Dean Witter. This ended up being cheerleading session on how to sell Dean Witter branded mutual funds. For one month every Dean Witter mutual fund manager touted their product in front of our class so that we would sell their mutual fund and not the other Dean Witter funds. We had to sell these mutual funds. If we didn't sell Dean Witter mutual funds, we didn't have a job.

I didn't last long as a stockbroker at Dean Witter. The first cut to my class was six months after we left the New York training session. Our class would be measured based on commissions generated, assets under management, and the number of premium accounts opened. I worked in South Florida and my clients didn't want to deposit their stock certificates into any institution (depression era survivors), nor did they want any account they had to pay $100 for. I didn't make it out of the bottom 25% of the class and was fired. It wasn't personal. I knew about the quotas, and I knew where I stood in my group of brokers.

Just remember that when you work with a stockbroker from a big Wall Street firm, they first work for the investment firm, selling whatever product management wants sold. Second, stockbrokers are working for themselves, trying to generate as much commission dollars as they can. And third, they work for you.

I then went to work for an insurance salesman who had

branched off into investments. His accounts had grown large enough that he wasn't able to spend the time he wanted doing sales. When I joined the company, he would bring in the clients, and I would service their accounts by picking asset allocations and specific investments for them. This was a <u>non-discretionary</u> type of business, meaning that we had to get client approval on all changes we made to their portfolio. I would review the clients' personal information, their current investments and asset allocation. Then make recommendations to asset allocation changes and specific investment changes once the account would transfer into the custodian that held our accounts. I would monitor and review all the client accounts the salesman had at least once a month. I kept all current client statements in my office so they were always close by. When all of the account statements came into the office, I would go over every page of every client statement. If there was something I wanted to address with the insurance salesman, I would write it down on a Post-it note and place it on the side of the statement.

I was responsible for most of the paperwork necessary to meet the regulatory requirements. I would have to do some client interaction, but that wasn't my best skill. I had one way of looking at investments and the salesman had another; therefore we would give out crossed signals to clients. The salesman and I actually complimented each other very well. We would moderate each other's eccentricities and we became an effective investment team.

The end started when the owner sold the insurance/investment company he owned to a larger publicly held insurance company. Then the firing started. Oh, I'm sorry, that's not politically correct; 'downsizing' and 'restructuring' was what they called it. The owner, partners and insurance salesman now had to make set revenue numbers. The lower positions on the office food chain, the average office workers, were being wholesale fired so that the owner, partners and insurance salesman would meet the projected EBITA (Earning Before Interest, Taxes and Amortization) revenue the new owners had set. Part of the agreement to sell the company stipulated that the sellers had to improve the bottom line by a set target to get the full sale price of the firm; it is called 'performance-based incentives'. If the EBITA amount was below the required number, the difference was taken away from the sale price of the firm. The owner, partners and insurance salesman would have money taken away from them. I guess they didn't like that idea. It got so bad that just before one Christmas, the original owner of the firm called a meeting in the lunch room to announce that there would be no more firings i.e. downsizing. The very next day several people were handed their pin slips, Merry Christmas!

My deal with the previous owner of the insurance company was that: "I only recommend and sell products that make money for the clients." I made that statement at my job interview with him, and he always remembered that declaration. He would proudly tell any client about my attitude and that that was what got me the job in the first place. That situation changed after he sold his company. I believed that revenues were taking priority over clients' personal investment objectives. The investment management side of the business was asked several times to produce more revenue to help shortfalls of revenue on the insurance side. The insurance salesman would sell annuity products to clients who I knew didn't need them. Annuities are the highest commission-paying investment we could sell. I had no part in those investment decisions except to execute what I thought were bogus trades that benefited the company more than the clients.

There were some other backroom 'soft money' advertising deals that really bothered me. A Goldman Sachs mutual fund wholesaler provided the insurance salesmen a box of polo shirts embroidered with our investment company name on the breast and Goldman Sachs name on the sleeve. Over the next few weeks we invested millions of dollars worth of our clients' money into Goldman Sachs Funds. This was in 2001 when the market and Goldman Sachs Funds were taking a huge downturn. For the next few months I pleaded monthly to sell all Goldman Sachs Funds on my monthly account reviews. I was finally told by the insurance salesman that we couldn't sell any of the Goldman Sachs mutual funds. I suggested moving the money to the Goldman Sachs money market, but I was told we couldn't to do that either. I then asked him, "Did you sell your soul for a box of shirts?" I was told to leave the meeting.

I then came up with a joke I would use to give the insurance salesmen a reality check when he did something I felt was questionable. The joke was, "When does a box of shirts cost over a million dollars (this referred to the total losses in Goldman Sachs Funds in our clients' accounts)?" I never got an answer from him, but I did ask that question several times to make the point: put client concerns before business concerns. I'm so ashamed that I accepted a shirt when they arrived. I ended up giving it away.

Another reason for me leaving the firm was that on June 3, 2002 I had an epiphany. This was the time India and Pakistan were casually talking about lobbing nuclear weapons at each other. I was always a believer in asset allocation as a viable portfolio management tool. What I realized was that a portfolio's asset allocation can't be cast into stone. It must be flexible to adjust for current market conditions. On June 4, 2002 I moved all of my personal clients, about one million dollars in assets, into money market. I sold off everything equity, mutual fund and bond. The DOW Jones Industrial Average closed around 9800 that day. Every one of my clients thanked me when I called to discuss the move.

My allocation model remained 100% money market until June of 2003. The Dow was around 9000 at this time, but it had dipped down below 8000 three times before heading back up. I think I added a little value and 'sleep at night comfort' to my clients over that time.

I called a meeting with the two salesmen in the office and told them about my revelation. They thought I was nuts. They accused me of being a hedge fund manager. I replied that I had changed my asset allocation, and that it was a smart and logical move in a downward-moving market. They made sure I knew that if I relayed this philosophy to any of their clients, I would be fired. They said that there was no research to back up my idea. I replied that all their clients were telling me one thing, they were tired of losing money month after month, and they repeatedly asked me to, "Stop the bleeding." A Wall Street phrase referring to ending the losses in an investment account.

On August 16th, 2002 I stayed late in my office. I emptied out my desk of personal things, made notes on all the client files on my desk, described how and where I'd saved my computer files, sent an email to all the office staff telling them I was leaving, turned my computer off and dropped my keys off at human resources. I regret not giving the firm two weeks' notice. I felt that they would make me work the two weeks, and that during those two weeks I could be accused of some impropriety that could be reflected on my permanent securities record.

American Asset Management, LLC was born. I decided to structure my company as a Register Investment Advisory firm. There was a lot more paperwork and compliance issues involved, but it was a much more transparent business entity with lots more disclosures to my clients. I would be able to charge a percentage of assets under management or a set fee to clients. I couldn't charge commissions on transactions, but the clients would have to pay for all executions, so price of trades was a big concern for me. I finally chose to be affiliated with Fidelity Investments as the custodian of my clients' accounts, a decision I do not regret.

I poured my heart and soul into my mission and vision statement for my company. I truly believe that an ethical foundation of putting clients' interests first makes sense. The compliance company I used had me make significant changes to these statements. I wanted my clients and prospective clients to know I believed in answering my own phone, I was concerned about their needs and if the company ever got so big that servicing their needs became difficult, I would accept no more clients. I have an idea of how big I want this company to be and once it got there I would stop taking on new clients.

I adopted the CFA Institute, formerly the Association for Investment Managements and Research (AIMR), ethical guidelines for my company. I believe in telling my clients that I have ethics and my business practices are stacked in their favor. I had actually joined the CFA Institute several years earlier because this was the only Wall Street organization I could find that really stressed ethics. They actually tested you on ethics if you wanted to become a Chartered Financial Analyst (CFA). I passed the ethics test, but the CFA test I've failed three times in a row. Needless to say it is a very difficult test. The failure rate for the CFA level II test in 2000 was 46%, 2001 was 54%, 2002 and 2003 it was 53% and the failure rate in 2004 was **68%**. These test results were posted by the CFA Institute in their 2006 Level I CFA Program Curriculum.

I had already decided that my investing strategies would be structured as guidelines rather than cast-in-stone rules. It makes my investment model flexible and adaptable to most investor's needs. I like to think of my investment strategies as safe enough so that clients can 'sleep soundly at night.' However, it can be very active management at times.

I closed **American Asset Management, LLC** down in 2005. There weren't enough assets under management to make it a viable entity. I made sure my clients had a place to put their investments before closing the books on my company. I thought that closing my company would have bothered me more, but I was OK. I learned a lot about investing and business in general while running my company. I relearned that I should never do sales/marketing again; I should leave that part of the business to the sales professionals.

I then went to work for Evergreen Investments, a wholly owned subsidiary of Wachovia Bank. My job was Portfolio Manager; I would manage the investment portfolios of trust clients. From day one the job just got worse and worse. On the first day of working at Evergreen Investments it was explained to me that the salesperson who sat in front of the trustee was my client, not the trustee, not the beneficiaries. A salesperson was my client. My investment choices for these trust accounts were an approved list of mutual funds, individual equities, and individual bonds. This list was further reduced by what the salesperson approved of and could explain to the clients; otherwise my bonus would suffer. That system of managing these trust accounts didn't sit well with me at all.

The reason for my quick departure from Evergreen Investments was that Wachovia Bank's trust department was undergoing a major restructuring. Evergreen Investments and Wachovia Bank were moving on to a new investment model which I thought was better than the previous one. What really concerned me was that they were going to triple the workload of the portfolio managers. I had about 450 trust investment accounts to manage and maintain when I started. I was barely keeping up with the current workload. By the end of 2006 I would have 1300 trust investment accounts. I don't know how Evergreen Investments and Wachovia Bank expected the portfolio managers to work that many accounts in any semblance a professional manner. Management was constantly telling us that this increase in workload was in the best interest of the client, but I couldn't see it myself. All I could see was how Wachovia Bank was going to save a bundle of money in payroll. Wachovia's new trust model didn't have many Evergreen products. It looked to me that Wachovia Bank was going to spin off or put Evergreen Investments up for sale sometime in the future.

I tried very hard to accept this new model, but in my heart I knew it was profit driven, not client driven. I was increasingly having a harder time getting up to go to work. I love finance and investing in a 'geeky' kind of way, I am also very passionate about it. I just wasn't excited about going to work. It was time; I called my parents and bounced the idea off of them about me leaving Evergreen. I wanted to be sure that I was thinking clearly. On June 11th I drafted a letter of resignation, and on June 12th I handed it to my team leader. I gave Evergreen Investments and Wachovia Bank a three-week notice period. On June 30th, 2006 I cleaned out my desk at the end of the day, handed in my security card and away I went. I had a big smile on my face, I was happy again.

I'm writing this background because I want you, the reader, to know why I work with investments on Wall Street. It's for all the right reasons, I hope. I want to help grow investors' wealth, to make a difference in people's lives; I want to educate others about finance and investments. I want to make retirement a little happier and more secure for the investors I work with.

I doubt that I will ever be a rich person in a material sense unless I marry a rich woman or win the lottery. I measure my personal wealth by my friends, my memories, my adventures, the scars on my body, the challenges I meet, and the new things that I learn. I measure my professional success in the finance arena by my ability to help grow wealth, personalizing investment solutions to meet specific needs, and looking far enough into the future to prepare well in advance for the changing times we will soon be living in. I make many compromises in my life, we all do, but I will not compromise when I invest other peoples' money!

I have worked on Wall Street for more than fourteen years, and I still lie in bed at the end of a hectic day and wonder if I made the right asset allocation and investment decisions in my clients' accounts. I review my reasoning for making the changes. I feel the weight of the decisions I made that day and the effects they will have on my clients' financial future. I know that behind each account and statement there is a real person or family who depends on me to do what is right for them. I know that my genuine concern for my clients and not being motivated to make money for myself keeps me making better investment decisions on their behalf. If the day comes where making money is my primary goal for working on Wall Street, I will quit this business without a second thought.

My personal investment motto is, 'Client First!'

My favorite investment saying, 'Buy when there's blood in the Street!'

My personal motto is, 'Limits were meant to be tested!'

Chapter 2

SCOTT'S NINE SIMPLE INVESTMENT GUIDELINES

The year was 1998. I was working with the insurance salesman and had been managing investment portfolios for about four years. I was at my office in a meeting with clients describing how I wanted to adjust their portfolios' asset allocation and what investment vehicles we would use to reach that allocation. The meeting was going pretty well. They seemed interested and open to the ideas that I was presenting to them. Then one of them asked a question that really rattled me. It was a simple question, and one which I should have been able to answer without thinking too much. I sat there horrified because I couldn't answer him. It was a simple question, yes, but with a very complicated answer. An answer that would entail every aspect of finance, economics and psychology.

The question was, "Scott, what are the investment rules you use to invest my money?"

My answer that morning was, "You know."

I was taught early in life that if you can't explain a process or theory to someone, you don't really know it yourself. I spent months working on the answer to that one simple question, and I will share that answer with you now.

There are always exceptions to any Wall Street rule, so I have decided to answer this question using a series of 'guidelines'. Guidelines give some wiggle room so you can fit them to each individual's need or situation. These guidelines are mine and have been tailored to my specific investment style. You will need to adapt them to you personal style. That may require you to add or subtract a few, but that's OK. Remember, investing is a very personal experience. Accept that fact and adapt this book to your own personal needs and style. If you do, you will be a much better investor.

You will always see my guidelines in print, never in stone, glass or metal, that way I can update, add or subtract them as I see fit. These guidelines, like investors, must be flexible. Wall Street is a very dynamic place; procedures and rules don't have a lot of time to collect dust. If you decide to plant roots on Wall Street, you will be trampled and crushed by the bulls and the bears.

1. BUY LOW/SELL HIGH

This is **THE** fundamental **GUIDELINE** of investing. I just thought I would remind you of how to make money on Wall Street. It seems like investors forgot the 'sell high' part of the rule. You have to follow through the entire investing process to make money: buying an investment, holding that investment for a period of time, and finally selling that investment. This guideline is at the heart of, or encompasses, every investment strategy, theory, calculation, and principle in the world of finance. The goal is profits!

Did you ever consider first selling high, and second, buying low? It's called a short sale and I'll discuss it later in the book.

2.   <u>MANAGE RISK BY ASSET ALLOCATION</u>

Asset allocation is the method used to decide the ideal mixture of what investments you should hold in your portfolio and what percentage of each asset class to own. I will cover this topic in more detail throughout this book. What are your assets? My guideline is that an asset is anything you own worth more than $5,000 including:

HARD ASSETS: you can see, feel and touch hard assets.

- Cash and Currency
- House
- Cars
- Land
- Art Work
- Wine Collection
- Business
- Planes
- Boats
- Jewelry

SOFT ASSETS: proof of ownership for soft assets is on a statement or certificate.

- Bonds
- Stocks
- Savings Account
- Retirement Plans
- Life Insurance
- Annuity

Since I am in the business of managing financial liquid assets, soft assets, I'll be primarily discussing investments in equity (stock), fixed income (bonds) and cash (money market funds). An easy way to describe my investment world is that proof of ownership is only in the form of a statement you receive from the custodian either monthly or quarterly. My investments have no physical form that you can touch and hold. I don't deal with debts, loans or payment obligations; this book will strictly address ASSETS only! That's why we spend so much time discussing asset allocation and not debt allocation. I'll take a moment to explain the investments in my universe in a little more detail.

Equity a.k.a. Stock

Owning equity or shares of a company's stock means that you own part of that company. Each company who issues shares of stock has a 'Transfer Agent'. It is the transfer agent's job to know on a daily basis who the equity owners are and how many shares of the company stock they own.

Being an equity owner of a company grants you certain rights, privileges, and obligations.

- You have the right to receive dividends that the board of directors declares. Dividends are usually paid on a quarterly basis, if paid at all.

- You have the privilege of having limited liability that the company you own is exposed to. This means that if the company you own stock in goes into bankruptcy, the creditors of the firm can't come after you personally, as an owner, for any debts of the firm. If the company is sued for any reason, you, as an equity owner, can't be added as a liable party to the claim. The maximum you can lose as an equity owner is the amount you paid for your shares.

- As an owner you also have the right/obligation to vote your shares when asked. This could be to decide the board of directors, the auditors of the firm or a proxy vote. I normally tell people that if they are happy with the movement of the stock price or the way current management is handling the firm's affairs, to vote the way that management is recommending. If you are unhappy with the stock performance or the decisions of the firm, vote against what management is recommending. Your vote usually won't make a big difference, but you should always vote your shares and know what the company is asking you to vote on.

Fixed Income a.k.a. bonds, a firm's paper, a debt instrument of the company.

When you pay money for a fixed-income investment, you are actually loaning money to a company, city government, state government, federal government, or any other entity. You just bought their debt or 'note'. Debt instruments are usually in the form of bonds. The issuing entity gets the sales proceeds at the time of issue. After that initial sale the notes or bonds are sold on a secondary market between investors.

In return for you loaning the entity money, the contract attached to the bond has the issuer agreeing to pay you interest at a set rate, interest will be paid on set dates and then the principal amount will be returned when the loan matures. There is more on this subject in the 'MAKING MONEY WITH BONDS' chapter.

Cash a.k.a. money market, saving account or checking account.

In this book cash will always be in a demand account, either a money market or savings account. It is called a 'demand account' because you have the right to access your money when you <u>demand</u> it i.e. request a withdrawal. This is the most liquid investment you can own other than the currency. This will usually be the lowest interest paying investment you will own due to the short-term nature of the investments.

Liquidity refers to the ability to sell an investment immediately without significant loss of value. If you <u>had</u> to sell your house today, you would receive far less than the fair market value. That is why your house is one of the most illiquid investments the average investor owns.

Currency: Dollar bills, nickels and dimes have a physical presence and therefore are not in my investment universe. Dollar bills and coins are also called 'Hard Assets' because you can see and hold them.

One other asset that isn't normally considered an investment is yourself and your family. <u>You</u> are probably the biggest asset you have. You insure your house and cars. Are your health and income stream insured? Health insurance is pretty straightforward. What about your income stream in case you are injured or suddenly become disabled? Can you and your family survive without you ever earning another paycheck again? Do you have a will and a living trust? Do you have enough assets to need a trust that ensures you actually pass on most of your assets to your heirs and not the government? You have protected your other hard assets, now it is time to think about protecting yourself! After finishing this book, get educated on insurance, but get only what you need. This is important!

3. JUST BEFORE THE FEDERAL OPEN MARKET COMMITTEE CHANGES THE DIRECTION OF INTEREST RATES, IT IS TIME TO ADJUST YOUR ASSET ALLOCATION.

Each time they meet, the Federal Open Market Committee (FOMC) controls the financial destiny of billions of people, most large companies around the world, and even every individual country. The FOMC control our perception of the financial health of the economy of the Unites States of America. The FOMC presents to the world a brief statement on their current take on the economy and which direction the huge machine called the United States economy is heading.

Every time the FOMC meets there are only three possible interest rate outcomes: increased interest rates, reduced interest rates, or interest rates kept at the current level. They do this by controlling The FED funds interest rate. This is the interest rate that member banks pay to borrow money overnight to meet their reserve requirements. This FOMC is the most watched, analyzed, critiqued, followed, and rumored about government entity in the world. This is a testament to the purchasing power of the US economy. It is no wonder so many analysts follow so few policy makers so intently.

The FOMC also has another tool at their disposal, but it is something they haven't used in a long time. They can change the percentage of required reserves on the demand deposits that banks have. Let's say a generic bank has one billion dollars of demand deposits. At the end of every day the bank must maintain somewhere around 4% or $40,000,000 in cash. If they don't have enough cash on hand, they borrow the balance from the FED to bring their cash up to the required reserve. The loan only lasts overnight and is repaid with interest the next day. The demand deposits are used to make long-term loans to the banks customers. If the FOMC raises the required reserve, then the bank have less money to loan to it customers.

I am a 'big picture' and 'concept' thinking investment manager. I define my 'big picture' strategy as covering all of your investment assets, not a small part of your portfolio. You need to look at your total wealth picture, and also your debt.

My simple strategy will require you to be more proactive than a 'buy and hold' investor. Buy and hold investing is a great tool which enables the big Wall Street brokerage and mutual fund companies to keep your money. My investment method is supposed to make major asset allocation changes no-brainers! I can't take the emotion out of these decisions or tell you what individual stocks or bonds will make money over the next two years, but I can help automate the asset-allocation decision, making the investment process a little easier.

WHAT TO DO WHEN THE FOMC IS RAISING INTEREST RATES

The FOMC generally raises interest rates to keep inflation under control in a strong economy. As a professional money manager I believe that an increasing interest rates environment is a great time for investing in equities. Stocks usually do better in a strong economy than a weak one. I believe that in this economic environment it is prudent to overweight equities and underweight bonds/fixed income in your asset allocation.

I have decided to do my own illustrations for this book. Not that I'm very good at it, I admit that I'm a horrible artist. I want you to focus on the general idea or concept I'm trying to get across. I don't want you to get fixated and wrapped up in the small details. This book is all about 'big picture ideas and concepts' not the fine print. The illustration above represents a seesaw that you would find at most playgrounds when you were a kid. One person would get on each side; they would adjust their positions to account for their different weight and then bounce up and down at play. On the right is **interest rates**, as interest rates move up and down, you can see the effect on the other side in the price that bond would now trade for in the open market. I'll go into the math in the chapter about making money with bonds.

In an increasing interest rate environment the value of your fixed income will go down. The total amount of fixed income in your asset allocation not only needs to be underweighted but also have the maturities shortened. The longer the maturity a bond has, the more the bond will be negatively impacted by an increasing interest rate environment. It is important to make these changes before interest rates start to increase:

- Sell the bonds you don't need for income to lock in the capital gains. You don't want to sell bonds for less or at a loss as interest rates increase.

- Hold the bonds that you need for income and can keep until maturity.

- The proceeds of the bond sales should be used to overweight the equity portion of your portfolio and to shorten your overall bond maturity, buying one to three-year bonds.

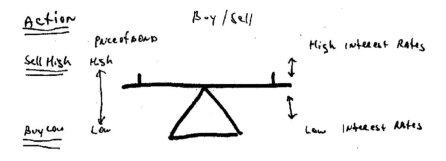

This illustration's big idea: **As interest rates increase the price of a bond declines, and as interest rates decline the price of a bond increases. Interest rates have the opposite effect on the price of bonds. Buy when interest rates are low and sell when interest rates are high.**

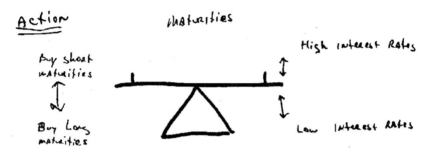

This illustration's big idea: When interest rates are high, buy long maturity bonds.. When interest rates are low, buy short maturities that you can hold until maturity.

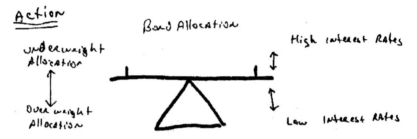

This illustration's big idea: When interest rates are high, you want to overweight the bond allocation in your portfolio. When interest rates are low, you want to underweight the bond allocation in your portfolio.

WHAT TO DO IN A LOWERING INTEREST RATE ENVIRONMENT

When the FOMC starts to lower interest rates, it generally indicates that inflation is not a big issue. The economy is cooling or slowing so the FOMC is trying to simulate the economy with cheaper money. This tells me that the economy is weak and needs a booster shot. It is time to lower equity allocations, raise fixed-income allocations, and lengthen maturities.

In an decreasing interest rate environment the total amount

of fixed income in your asset allocation not only needs to be overweighted but also have the maturities extended as far out as you can stand. The longer the maturity a bond has, the more the bond will be positively impacted by a decreasing interest rate environment. It is important to make these changes:

- Buy the bonds you need for income to lock in today's high interest rate. Different bonds will make their interest payments in different months. When you buy interest-bearing bonds, consider different bonds that pay in all twelve months of the year. This will prevent large fluctuations in receiving interest income.

- The bonds that you need for income should have maturities as far out as you can live with. Thirty-year bonds are better than ten-year bonds.

- Now is the time to overweight the fixed income and underweight the equity portion of your portfolio.

The chapter on making money with bonds will cover all of this material in much more greater detail using simple math.

HOW DO YOU KNOW WHEN TO MAKE THESE ASSET ALLOCATION CHANGES TO YOUR PORTFOLIO?

Interest rates are speculated on and talked about in the press every time the FOMC gets ready to meet. The FOMC meets at predetermined dates every year so there is rarely an unscheduled meeting or rate change. The FOMC uses several economic indicators to make their decisions. Inflation, Gross Domestic Product, and Per Capita Income are a few of the main measurements that they use to make decisions on interest rates. If you can't bear to make these changes, find a professional advisor who can and will do it for you.

With all the hype in the press it shouldn't be too hard to

keep track of these FOMC meetings, along with what the press thinks the outcome of the meeting will be. All you need to be concerned about is a change from increasing rates to lowering rates or vice versa. If you want to slowly make the changes that I suggest, then that's OK. The number one thing to remember is to do what is right and comfortable for you. It's just not worth losing sleep over having a too aggressive or too volatile portfolio.

Don't look for instant gratification with my method. It may take a while for the markets to change or react to the interest rate changes. If the interest rates decrease and the markets continue to climb, take comfort that you didn't move all of your equity investments into fixed income. Take comfort in knowing that you have adopted an investment method; there are millions out there who are clueless and have no plan for investing their finances whatsoever.

4. IF AN INVESTMENT GOES UP OVER 40% OR DOWN TO 15%, IT'S TIME TO RE-EVALUATE HOLDING THAT INVESTMENT IN THE PORTFOLIO.

When you make an investment in an equity, bond, ETF, or mutual fund, you pick the entry price; that is the price you pay for the investment. At the same time you should pick an exit price; one exit price on the upside and another exit price on the downside. As a general rule of thumb I use 40% upside and 15% downside price movements to set my exit price. If the investment price movement is volatile, you should consider using 50% upside and 25% downside to set your exit price. If the investment price movement is stable, you should consider using 25% upside and 10% downside to set your exit price. You will need to write down that exit price and keep a list with all exit prices for all of the investments in your portfolio, reviewing it frequently. Now that doesn't mean you will automatically sell at the exit price, but it will trigger a sell review.

A sell review should make you look at the investment from scratch. Would you buy that investment at the current price in the portfolio? If the answer is "no", then it is time to sell that investment and bank the profits. If the answer is "yes", you will have to set a new exit price. In the case of an investment going up 40%, you need to consider:

- How long it took to get reach the exit price.

- How quickly the price moved up. There may be a pullback in price where you can sell it now and buy it back at a lower price. The price may just sit at this higher level for a while; consider another investment with more current price appreciation. I normally watch an equity investment for several months to years before buying. I like to know the company, get a general idea on how the equity price moves, and how various financial climates affect the price.

- Did the price move up slowly? You may want to keep this one and just reset the exit price.

In the case of an investment going down 15%, triggering a sell review:

- I look at how the investment has been trading.

- Does this look or feel like a short-term dip?

- Did news come out that adversely affects the company?

- Are there any fundamental changes in the company since you bought it?

- Look at the volume of shares trading during the downturn; was it higher or lower volume? If it was lower volume on the down days when the price dropped, it could be the case of more sellers than buyers. If the price goes down in heavy volume, it could be a general market perception that this decline will continue for a while.

Other indicators I look at when making a sell decision:

a.   Management changes

b.   Projected earnings issued by the company

c.   Analysts downgrading the company

d.   Has the industry materially changed?

e.   Are there new competitors?

f.   Are there fewer competitors?

g.   Are there new products out on the market that will replace the product made by the company you are invested in?

h.   Has the economy changed?

You can make the sell review as simple or as complex as you want. What does your gut instinct tell you? There are no tried and true formulas for 100% accurate investment analysis. I believe that many trades come down to gut instincts and 'The Balls' to make the trade. I almost always wait a day to trade after making a big investment decision. I really do '**sleep on my decisions**.' I find that my mind works on problems for me while I sleep. Sometimes I come up with different ideas or ways to solve a problem, or I always have a much stronger conviction to follow the path I had chosen after a good night's sleep. If there were one guaranteed investment rule to consistently make huge profits, someone would have developed it, and by now they would be ruling the world.

This is a very psychologically driven area of our lives. It pits our primal emotions of greed, power, wealth, ego fulfillment and need to survive over our rivals, real or perceived. We work to psyche out our opponents with locker-room lies on the performance of our portfolios, ridiculous claims of exorbitant returns, and stupid displays of wealth or power. Some people in this industry even start to believe these lies and set out to achieve their objectives with extremely speculative investments. Not a good basis for investing, and it shows as people's lives and companies crash and burn on the nightly news.

The sell decision is far harder to make than the decision to buy. When you sell an investment, that's the end of all possibilities. It's the closing point of this investment. No more possibilities. No more possible gains. No more losses. The final tally is at hand. You take the end price you sold the investment for, subtract what you paid for it and hopefully the number will be positive, which means you made money!

My father reminded me recently of one of his preferences about selling an investment. He liked to hold an investment until it doubled, then sell off his original investment amount, keeping the balance invested. He liked the idea that if the investment totally crashed, he had already taken back the initial investment amount and didn't lose any money. He always kept part of his winning positions as a reminder of why he was investing. He would eventually sell them, but only when he was ready and always at a profit. I'm not sure that will work all that well for me and my investing style. I have tracked his portfolio for him, and it does seem to work for him.

5. <u>INVEST IN A COMPANY THAT HAS PRODUCTS AND CUSTOMERS</u>

One of the best investment mottos I ever read went something like this: "If you like the companies that you shop at or you use their services, then invest in that company." I can't remember where I read this motto, but it brings home the products and customers idea. The company you shop at may have boring everyday products. The company may not be the in the current 'hot industry', but over the long haul you will monitor this company every time you shop there.

Another idea along the same lines is that I like to invest in the best company in the industry, or at least the top tier companies in their line of business. Own a company that is going to be in business next year. Time and time again I have to reminding myself, on those rare occasions I go shopping, to spend that little bit of extra money for the best quality available. You are rarely dissatisfied when you spend that extra money on quality, so apply that same philosophy to the quality of the investment you buy. Carrying that idea one step further, apply it to the quality of the investment advice you decide to listen to.

BUDGET TRUCK RENTAL STORY

I recently moved to the Little Rock, Arkansas area to work as a portfolio manager. Unfortunately, the following story is true. Below is the actual letter I wrote to the management team of Budget Truck Rental and the board of directors of Avis, which owns Budget Truck Rental.

Ms XXXXXXXXX, EVP

Budget Headquarters

6 Sylvan Way

Parsippany NJ 07054

RE: Rental Agreement # 02128015

Hello Ms. XXXXXXX,

I've had a horrific Budget Truck Rental and Budget Truck Rental Customer Service experience.

I went to Budget Truck Rental online and reserved a 16' truck, a hand dolly and two-dozen pads. I called several days before I was scheduled to pick up these items. The lady at the pick-up location said everything on my reservation would be there when I arrived to pick them up. I emphasized that I really needed a 16' truck, and she said that a 16' truck would be there. This wasn't the case. My 16' truck ended up being a 24' truck. The hand dolly I reserved ended up being an appliance dolly. The two-dozen pads were nowhere to be found. Not one item that I had ordered online or received a verbal confirmation for was available.

The location I picked up the truck:

Budget SRB8

10246 Atlantic Blvd

Jacksonville, FL 32225

You probably wouldn't be hearing from me if this were all that I had problems with, but the truck that your company rented me was a filthy deathtrap. The air conditioner didn't work. The radio didn't work. The instrument panel lights worked sometimes. The exterior lights wouldn't turn off at times. At around 58 miles per hour the truck shook so badly that on two separate occasion truckers pulled up next to me, honked their horns and pointed to the back of the truck.

Like I said, the interior, where I spent all of my time while traveling in the truck, was a pigpen. Garbage was strewn all over. There were footprints on the inside of the windshield. The windshield was chipped. The driver's seat was torn up. There was graffiti down the entire driver's side of the back end. There were tears in the metal of the back end where I put my belongings. The front end of the truck looked like it had been in a demolition derby.

*To say that I am very angry and upset about this near-death truck rental experience is an understatement. The only experience that was worse than driving this filthy deathtrap truck was how I was treated by the Budget Customer Services department. All the customer service representatives would say while I had the truck was that I had to close out the contract before they could address my concerns. No one would take ownership to solve MY problem. The customer service motto seemed to me to be, 'The customer is always wrong! Lie extensively to cover Budget's ass!' After several calls, one lasting more than an hour, trying to convince my only contact, your customer service department, I gave up. Frustrated, pissed off and feeling like I had been gigantically **RIPPED-OFF** and that I was a **SUCKER!***

The location that I returned the truck was:

Kings One Stop

23724 Hwy 10

Little Rock, AR 72223

The first thing the guy did at the return location was to take the truck out of service. He drove the truck and confirmed the wild vibrations along with the horrible general condition of this truck. He then scheduled the truck to be towed to be service location; he wasn't about to drive that deathtrap truck again.

When I called the Budget Customer Service department after

34

I closed out my contract they said there was nothing they would/could do because I closed out the truck rental contract. I asked to speak to a supervisor and she said that there was nothing Budget was willing to do to address my concerns about the horrific truck rental I experienced or any compensation for having to use a larger diesel-fuel-guzzling truck and the longer trip miles to accommodate that larger truck. I asked if there was anyone else I could speak to and I was referred to Mr. Shawn Polk, the customer service manager. I have left him multiple voicemails and have not heard back from him.

Let me tell you what I do for a living. I'm the Investment Analyst/Portfolio Manager for an investment company. I handle all of the investing activities from stock selection to asset allocation for all of the firm's accounts, a substantial amount. Besides that I'm finishing up a book titled, Making Dollar$ and Sense on Wall Street. You can read an outline at my website www.sgoodrick.com. I have no leverage in the truck market, but I have extensive contacts and I'm a center of influence in the equity and capital markets.

I'm going to mention this horrific Budget Truck Rental experience in my book. I have the perfect place in my book to discuss this life-threatening experience and will be happy to tell all the nasty details in very colorful terms. I'm going to mention this horrific Budget Truck Rental experience at every stop on the media tour that will follow the release as I make my way around the country on the book tour. I'm going to mention this horrific Budget Truck Rental experience to every investment professional I come in contact with. I'm going to mention this horrific Budget Truck Rental experience to every investment analyst who follows your company. I'm going to mention this horrific Budget Truck Rental experience at every possible chance to my friends, neighbors and anyone else who will listen. In general I will cost

Budget Truck Rental far more than the rental amount received from the company I work for, who paid for my move.

I have a very hard time figuring out how people can justify working for a company who screws over and rips off their clients. If I did that, I would be out of business in a very short period of time. I find so much value in helping people achieve their financial goals. I guess your employees get a thrill out of taking advantage of people. That is a very sad corporate culture, and an even sadder way to conduct business.

I hope that someone someday will take ownership of the problems I have conveyed,

Dana Scott Goodrick

On January 11th, 2008 Budget Truck Rental Issued Check number 3596730 for $562.38 to me. That was the entire cost of my rental contract with them. The point of this story! If I wasn't worried about saving my employer $50.00, the difference of the rental price with Penski Truck Rental, I believe I could have avoided all of the problems with this move.

6. <u>DON'T FOLLOW THE HERD</u>

This is a direct result of the NASDAQ meltdown in the early 2000's or the real estate/mortgage bust of the 2007. Greed, media hype, perceived competition and desperation can blind otherwise very conservative investors. Investors get that horrible feeling of 'Missing the boat' on a hot stock. They are caught up in the 'herd mentality' to jump on board any similar type of investment. These investors start to make really bad financial decisions. They are caught in the 'Buy! Buy! Buy!' hype they hear on television or read in the papers. Another reason it may be a bad investment decision to follow the herd is that the same people who were screaming 'Buy! Buy! Buy!' aren't around or won't tell you when to 'sell'. Have you ever heard those same people that yell 'Buy! Buy! Buy!' yelling 'Sell! Sell! Sell!'?

You won't hear 'SELL! SELL! SELL!' Whoever says this always loses. In a typical non-institutional investor's eyes, most sales are always at too low a price and always at the wrong time. Investors rarely complain about a purchase because the possibilities are endless. The sale is an end of all possibilities.

I'm a contrarian and damn proud of it! I also do not read the *Wall Street Journal*, *Barons*, *Forbes*, *Money* or *Fortune*. If I did read these fine publications, I would be using the same information to form the same opinions as every other person working on Wall Street. I do not want that!

As a 'big picture' 'forward-thinking' 'concepts' thinker, I want my own ideas to form about companies in my brain, not a biased story from a reporter who may be trying to push their own opinion or point of view. I spend at least one hour a day reading a wide variety of Internet-based finance and international news websites. I don't have a television in my home; I found that I would just sit in front of it and zone out when I could be doing other productive projects with my time. I read a book on finance and the next book of whatever I want to read. Currently I've been on a classics kick. *Moby Dick* is my next book after I finish *The Wisdom of Crowds* by James Surowieki. I think the best book I have ever read is *The World is Flat* by Thomas L. Friedman. Homer's *The Odyssey* would be a close second. I'm explaining this to you so that you know where my ideas come from, or indeed where they don't come from.

I like the idea that I will have a different opinion than others on 'The Street'. Having a different point of view of the markets gives me an edge. If I hear a few money managers talking about buying an investment or that an investment is a ' 'must-have' or 'a fist pounding buy' in Wall Street lingo, I'm looking to sell, Sell, SELL! Boutique stocks are 'must-have positions in your portfolio' and most money managers are touting them on the investment cable channels and other news outlets. If most money managers are buying a certain company or holding it in their accounts, they are acting with a herd mentality. There is safety in numbers. These money managers can always defend that position by saying, "Well, everyone else on the street owns it." What a load of crap. What's worse is that the clients actually buy that garbage.

I am a member of the CFA Institute. I receive their monthly magazine and go to some really good meetings where I have been educated by Federal Reserve Bank presidents, CEOs, CFOs and large brokerage firms' chief economic and research analysts. The insight that these speakers have given really gives me a new outlook on how I perceive our industry and investing. At the same time, I know their agenda for speaking at all of these meetings is to put their firm, research or product in a favorable position so we, as investment managers, might use the investment service or product they are talking about.

7.   CAPITAL GAINS TAXES ARE DESIRABLE

Having To Pay Taxes Equal Profits!

As an investment manager I can either create profits or losses for my clients. I firmly believe that it is my job to create profits and **make my clients pay taxes!** Investing has changed radically over the past few years. I think that as the equity and bond markets become even more liquid, more investment professionals will have to lock in gains as they become available. The old adage of 'Buy and Hold' may be changed to 'Buy and Bank Profits'. It appears that this has been happening more and more. The markets seem to be moving in shorter cycles of highs and lows.

When I worked at a retail firm, we needed the client's approval on all the trades. I would recommend to clients that they needed to sell a position that had run up in value. The client had a substantial capital gain in that position and I wanted to 'bank that gain!' The client came back to me saying that their accountant didn't want them to pay capital gains taxes and refused to do the trade. Usually, a few months later I would call those same people back after the profitable position had gone down in value and was now below what they paid for it. I would ask the client if they are now ready to sell that same position for a loss. They would say "NO!" They didn't want to sell an investment for a loss and their accountant didn't want them to sell an investment for a gain. Why were they investing?

I believe it is the accountant's job to find ways for the client not to pay the taxes on the profits and capital gains I create for my clients. Capital gains taxes mean that the accountant is going to have to do more work and find other places in your finances to lower your tax bill. Accountants hate profits! It makes them work! Don't EVER ask an accountant for investment advice. That's the reason I don't handle non-discretionary accounts any longer. Discretionary accounts are ones where the client signs a contact allowing the money management firm to buy and sell in their accounts without any consultation.

Taxes are the price of investment success! Don't whine to me about taxes. You should be proud and tell all your fiends that Scott made me pay a huge tax bill! Yes, there are ways to lessen the effect of taxes, and I do try to use them. One way I do this is by doing my most aggressive trading in tax-deferred accounts, like retirement accounts. Another way is to invest in an equity that pays a high dividend in a non-retirement account. It doesn't have to be fancy to work. It just takes a little planning and staying abreast of the current changes in the tax codes.

8. EXCLUDE DYSFUNCTIONAL ASSET SECTORS FROM YOUR PORTFOLIO

I know my compliance company will cringe when they read this, but I will never own an airline or railroad stock in any of the accounts I manage. I have added telecomm, Internet providers, and telephone companies to that list until they get their act together, lower their debt load and a few more go out of business. I just can't see investing in an industry that is dying, is unprofitable, or working off a failed business model.

I have been looking at the tobacco industry as a dying industry. I personally think it will happen, but there still may be some profits to be made in this business before it goes. My job is to make people money. I try not to look at investments from a moral standpoint. I'm an ex-smoker and I tried for years to quit. I feel very lucky to have been smoke-free for twenty years. If I feel that a tobacco firm can provide my clients with a high return on their investment I will take it. If a client asks not to invest in a sin company: tobacco, alcohol, firearm defense manufacturer, etc., I will follow their wishes. That's another reason to write an Investment Policy Statement (IPS) for every discretionary account you have. The Investment Policy Statement (IPS) should detail any restrictions on what can be bought in the account.

9. <u>SET UP A SCHEDULE OF ROUTINE PORTFOLIO REVIEWS</u>

As an investor I review all of my personal assets on a monthly/quarterly/yearly basis. You should be receiving, at a minimum, quarterly statements or reports on all of your investment and retirement accounts. When these brokerage and retirement account statements come in the mail, I put them in a dedicated pile on my desk at home. When I have received all of the statements, it is time to get started with the review.

MONTHLY REVIEW

My monthly review is pretty basic. I check the name and account numbers on all of the investment statements. I compare last month's statement to this month's statement to see if my account has gained or lost value. I review any changes to the portfolio. The important part is to spend some time and review the transactions. The transaction section is usually the last section on the statement, just before those pages of really small disclaimer-filled type that no one reads. The transaction section tells you if dividends and interest payments were received into the account. The transaction section tells you if money has been deposited into or withdrawn from the account. What investments were bought or sold, and if any charges or fees were applied to the account. Basically, all of the things that informed investors need to know. If something is wrong, it can usually be quickly fixed by a phone call.

QUARTERLY REVIEW

I like to do a spreadsheet on all of my accounts for my quarterly review. It doesn't have to be an elaborate spreadsheet. List asset classes in a vertical column on the spreadsheet: money market, short-term bonds, long-term bonds, growth stocks, growth and income stocks, aggressive growth stocks, foreign stocks, then leave a few blank rows and put in a TOTAL class. That should cover the basics and you can get as involved as you like. Starting at the top of a column and going horizontally list all of the accounts you have. I also like to list the account numbers so that when I print this out I have all of them in one place. This may take several lines to get all of the information listed. When you have put in all the accounts on the spreadsheet, leave a few blank columns and put in a TOTAL and PERCENT column all the way to the right.

	A	B	C	D	E	F	G	H	I	J	K	L	M	N	O
1			AUGUST 2006												
3	ACCOUNT NUMBERS	514-96478214	213-874653	1587332	589744233		1587334			ASSET CLASS TOTAL		ASSET CLASS PERCENTAGE			
4	CUSTODIAN	E TRADE	FIDELITY	EMPLOYER 401K	SAVING		CHECKING								
6	FIXED INCOME														
7	MONEY MARKET	$442			$2,356		$7,251			$24,607		8.52%			
8					$15,000 EMERGENCY FUND										
9	BONDS <1 YEAR	$3,212								$3,212		1.11%			
11	BONDS >1 YEAR, <10 YEARS	$2,629								$2,629		0.88%			
13	BONDS >10 YEARS, <20 YEARS	$4,378								$4,378		1.52%			
15	BONDS >20 YEARS	$12,584								$12,584		4.36%			
18	EQUITY														
19	GROWTH	$8,964			$56,542					$65,506		22.68%			
21	GROWTH & INCOME	$64,231			$6,321					$70,552		24.43%			
23	MID CAP	$7,523			$22,389					$29,912		10.36%			
25	SMALL CAP	$2,314			$22,753					$25,067		8.68%			
27	INTERNATIONAL	$44,787			$5,712					$50,499		17.48%			
30	OTHER														
32	REITS			$8,734											
34	OPTIONS			$0											
37	ACCOUNT TOTALS	$150,964	$8,734	$113,717	$17,356		$7,251			$288,846		100.00%			
39					LAST MONTHS TOTAL					$284,577					
41					GAIN/LOSS					$4,269					

Now it's time to fill in the blanks. Remember to add the mutual funds and Exchange Traded Funds (ETF) into the applicable asset class. Once that is done you will need to total the rows down and columns across. If you don't know how to do that, get a book, you need to know how to work with spreadsheets.

NOTE: notice that the current 401k plan assets are all in most aggressive tax-producing equity investments for a long-term investor.

Compare your statements with the spreadsheet. Make sure that the account totals are very close, within 1%, of your investment statement's total account value. If not, fix it, this has to be right or everything will be incorrect. If the columns are correct, then you now have to make totals for your asset classes. Make sure that you total this column. This total will be used to figure out the percentages for asset classes. You can do this with the following formulas in the PERCENT column:

=SUM (value of asset class total to right/value of total of all asset class combined at bottom of row on right)

Make sure you highlight the PERCENT column and format the cells to percentage with two decimal places. You should also total the PERCENT column to make sure it adds up to 100. If it doesn't, your formula isn't right somewhere. If everything looks correct, make sure you **SAVE** the spreadsheet. You can always add a new sheet and copy the original sheet over, update the data and save the spreadsheet.

Now compare last quarter to this quarter. Are there any big changes in value or percentage? Did any asset class grow enough that you need to rebalance the portfolio? Rebalancing is the act of taking a portfolio in which one or more asset classes have over or under-performed the other investments, selling a portion of an over-performing asset class to buy into an under-performing asset class in the portfolio. The aim of this is to bring your portfolio back to your desired asset allocation. This usually means selling some of the winners and buying the losers. Kinda like buying low, under-performing positions and selling high, over-performing positions. Sound familiar? This is another easy no-brainer that should improve your performance.

I normally rebalance my personal portfolio four times a year, but if my portfolio has an accelerated month where one class really grows, I will rebalance my portfolio then. Transaction costs should be taken into consideration in portfolio rebalancing. The larger the dollar value of the portfolio you have, the more you should rebalance. I know of several billion-dollar pension plans that rebalance on a weekly basis. Notice that rebalancing doesn't sell the entire position; it is only a portion of the positions inside your portfolio.

YEARLY REVIEW

You should have at least one major financial review every year. This should involve your financial advisor along with your CPA or tax preparer, trust administrator, and personal lawyer. Who attends this annual review will depend on the size of your investment portfolio. The larger the portfolio, the larger the number of professionals who need to attend. If your portfolio is less than $1,000,000, your financial advisor and CPA need to attend. Over $1,000,000 and your entire personal professional management team need to attend.

If you do the annual review at the beginning of the year when all of your investment tax information is prepared using end of year documents, you can kill two birds with one stone in this meeting: investment review and personal taxes. The investment and performance information you go over at the annual review should be prepared by your financial advisor. Your advisor should prepare, at a minimum, the following information for each of your accounts:

- Your investment return for each account and for your total assets for the previous year, taking into effect contributions, withdrawals, and fees. This should be presented both in numerical and graph form. Make sure you get previous year, three-year, five-year and since account inception performance graphs, which contain the benchmark index you are tracking your portfolio against. The most common is the S&P 500.

- Realized gains and losses for the previous year. THIS IS NEEDED FOR TAXES.

- Unrealized gains and losses. This shows you each investment purchase price and current market price and the gain or loss if sold.

- Your current asset allocation in a pie chart by asset class for each account you have, and also a chart of all of your investment accounts combined.

- How much you paid the advisor the previous year. YOU MAY BE ABLE TO DEDUCT THIS AMOUNT FROM YOUR TAXES.

- What the advisor and the advisor's firm are anticipating economically for the upcoming year.

- What changes the advisor plans to make to take advantage of the market changes over the next year, and they should have specifics.

- If you have individual bonds. Have a graph or listing of maturity, dates and another showing call dates. And another graph showing credit quality by dollar amounts,

For the annual review you need to share with your investment advisor any important financial changes you have experienced over the past year, and any future known changes. These may include:

- Changes in your income

- Changes in employment

- Any large known cash flows coming to you: a settlement or

bonus.

- Any large known cash flow going out: college for child, any major purchase over $5,000.

Here's the way I worked this monthly/quarterly/annual review out with my clients at my former RIA firm. When I opened an investment account I got a list of all of the accounts the client had, even if I didn't manage or consult on those accounts. When I got back to my office, I prepared a three-ring binder for them. I made dividing pages with tabs labeled for all of their investment accounts, and a few extra dividing pages just in case the client wanted to add some other information or leave something out. I included a three-hole punch so my client could put holes in all of the paperwork I wanted them to put in this folder. I put the binder and three-hole punch in a box and express-mailed the package to my client's residence.

I liked to meet with my clients after they received their first investment account statement. I did a very detailed investment statement review, I wanted my clients to know and get comfortable with all the information on their investment statement. I showed them how to put in all of their investment statements in the front of each tabbed area and trade confirmations in the back of the same area.

I personally went over the first set of quarterly reports I sent to my clients. I made sure they were using the record-keeping system I went over with them at the first-month statement review. If I couldn't go over the quarterly reports in person, then I did this process over the phone. I described the contents of each page on the quarterly report, where that information came from and what it meant to them. The quarterly package I sent covered almost all of the information I listed for the yearly review. I normally met with my clients several times a year to stay current on their financial situation and to convey where I saw the markets and their accounts heading.

CONCLUSION

These are <u>my</u> INVESTMENT guidelines. They are how <u>I</u> have taken control of <u>my</u> finances and the finances of my clients. They may not all work for you. If they don't make sense to you, come up with your own guidelines and send a copy to me. I may have missed something, you never know.

Chapter 3

MY VIEW ON ASSET ALLOCATION AND MY DYNAMIC ASSET ALLOCATION MODEL

" **A**sset allocation is the concept of **determining** and **maintaining a plan** of investments in terms of a chosen mix of investments in different assets."

That definition comes from Wikipedia, and I think it's pretty good.

Determining your intitial asset allocation is the first part of this dynamic process. I use the word 'dynamic' because the process of asset allocation never stops, it mearly adjusts for various conditions such as: age of the investor, experience of the investor, time until the investor retires, the current market conditions, direction of interest rates and the dollar amount of investments you are working with. Once you determine the asset classes and their percentage allocation of your asset allocation, you will then need to determine the actual investments you will to use to meet the asset allocation.

Once you have your intital asset allocation and the investments purchased to achive your asset allocation, now you need to create and **maintain a plan** to keep your porfolio within the selected asset allocation ranges you have set. This process is called 'rebalancing', it brings your investment portfolio's asset allocation back to the initial asset allocation mix. Over time some investments will grow faster than others. Some investments will go down in value. That's the nature of Wall

Street. Rebalancing in effect is selling some of the winning positions and reinvesting in the losers. Harvesting profits and nurturing underperformers today because today's underperformers may be next year's winners! I've read studies that indicate the more reblalancing you do, the better the performance of the portolio. I do my rebalancing quarterly unless my account has really moved away from my initial asset allocation by over 5% in any one asset class. On some larger accounts I manage, I may rebalance monthly or twice a monthly. Reviewing is the practice of setting a firm schedule of personal/portfolio/investment evaluation.

Assets can be divided into many different classes, but for this book I will divide assets into three basic classes: equities, fixed income and cash, and short-term liquid cash assets otherwise known as money market instruments. When I refer to 'cash', I mean a money market account.

Equity shares are ownership interests in a particular company. This asset class can be broken down so many different ways that they become blurred. Equities can be divided into subclasses:

- Market Capitalization (market capitalization = number of equity shares outstanding X stock price). The main subclasses of market capitalization are: large capitalization (large-cap), middle-sized capitalization (mid-cap), small capitalization (small-cap) and very small capitalization (micro-cap).

- Industry categories like: financial, auto, chemical, retail.

- Growth and Income stocks pay a dividend and appreciate in price, while Growth stocks don't pay a dividend and only appreciate in value.

- Cyclical (affected by the cyclical growth and contraction of our economy) or non-cyclical.

- <u>Location</u>.   Where the companies are located is another subclass: domestic (inside the USA), foreign (outside the USA), international (both foreign and domestic), emerging markets, European Union, Asia, Asia ex-Japan.   Is a domestic company that does most of its business overseas a domestic or international stock?

The Wall Street experts can't even agree on a definition for large-cap, mid-cap and small-cap companies. The experts are usually mutual fund managers who want to create a definition that matches their investment style, and they will adjust what size they think market capitalization should be to meet their needs. For simplicity in this book, when I refer to an equity, it will be a large-cap company that has products and customers. It is one that will be in business several years down the road, although who really knows? Think of companies that make up the Dow Jones Industrial average, names like Caterpillar, Intel, Dupont, Microsoft or Home Depot to name but a few. That's not to say that mid and small-cap stocks don't have a place in your portfolio, but first we need to focus on the investment basics. We need to build a strong foundation of knowledge and stable investments.

THE STANDARD WALL STREET ASSET ALLOCATION MODEL

To see how different my investment model is you need to know what model most Wall Street firms use to determine asset allocation. It's called the 'Investment Pyramid'. The pyramid has a large, strong foundation built on large and sturdy rocks. As the pyramid gets taller it tapers in until ending in a point. The large, strong, and sturdy rocks or investments at the bottom of the investment pyramid will have little risk and are not volatile in price. As you move up the pyramid, the investments will increase in risk, which equates into price volatility. These investments should also decrease in the total percentage of your portfolio. At the top of the investment pyramid are the riskiest part of your portfolio and also the smallest percentage of your overall portfolio. Keep IN mind, if you build your pyramid with only the riskiest price-volatile investments available, your pyramid will be top heavy and could very easily collapse!

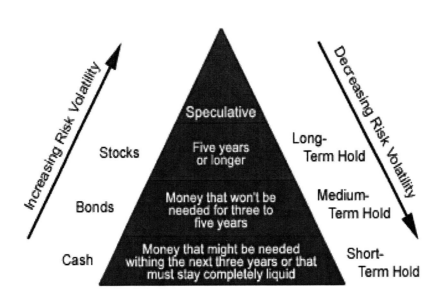

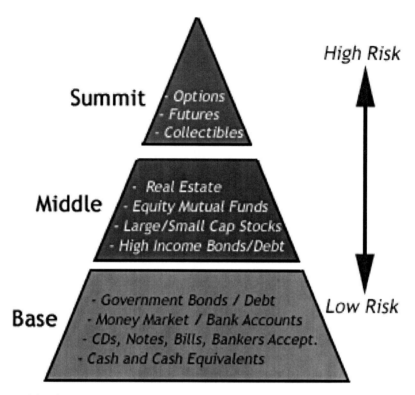

This is a very easy investment model to describe and visualize, no wonder most investment salespeople use it. What it lacks is anyway to adjust the asset allocation for changing market conditions or the aging of the investment portfolio owner. I believe that this is a very good model to collect your assets and keep them at a brokerage firm. It is also simple for financial salespeople to explain very quickly and without any formal investment education.

You meet with your brokerage salesperson to set your asset allocation and that's it. This investment model of picking the pyramids is in effect making your asset allocation 'cast in stone'. You no longer need to talk to that salesperson because you know what your portfolio will look like. More importantly, that salesperson doesn't need to talk to you again until they have another product to sell you. They are off selling their model to the next person and the next.

In my investment model I use age, investment experience, time to retirement, and amount of assets to invest to determine the asset allocation of a portfolio. Then to tactically adjust asset allocation I use the current direction of interest rates set by the Federal Open Market Committee (FOMC). This is the interest rate that the regional Federal Reserve Bank charges member banks for funds borrowed overnight. Banks and credit unions are required by law to hold in reserve a set percentage of all money held in their customers' demand accounts (checking and saving) as cash in a vault somewhere. The member banks use this overnight loan to increase their cash on hand to meet the required reserve on all demand deposits held at the bank. This allows for cash to be available for withdrawal, on demand, by the customers of the bank. The current required reserve is somewhere around 4%.

CAUTION: USELESS INFORMATION

The reserve requirement is a law from the days when there were many small one-branch banks. Before savings accounts were insured by some guarantying agency like the SPIC, and when the main mode of transportation was the horse! If a rumor started that a particular bank was in trouble of going out of business due to making bad loans, many nervous savings account holders would **RUN** down to the bank and withdraw all of their money. All banks made long-term loans with their customers' savings and didn't have enough cash in the vault to handle such a large-scale cascade of withdrawals. This would usually cause the bank to shut down to raise more cash or go out of business. This is where the phrase, 'run on the bank' came from. The people who didn't run to the bank and immediately withdrew their savings would often lose their savings if the bank closed. This rumor of a certain bank going under was also a commonly used tool to put rival banks out of business. Now most savings accounts are insured for the first $100,000 of cash.

BACK TO THE TOPIC

Why does the FMOC change interest rates?

I like to use a visual imagery to describe concepts or answers. To answer that question I visualize a straight set of railroad tracks traveling to the horizon in the central plains states. On these railroad tracks is a freight train laboring forward.

- This train is so long that the train stretches all the way to the horizon.

- I use the freight train as a symbol of the dynamic US economy.

- This train is moving on railroad tracks which symbolize the factors affecting our economy that the FOMC uses to make interest rate changes to FED funds, mainly inflation and worker productivity.

Our economy is so large that a very long train will have to be visualized, somewhere around twenty miles long. Our economy is made up of many different industries so there are many different types of container cars that make up this huge freight train.

Some of the different container cars on this train are:

- Boxcars filled with all of the industrial output of all industries in our economy.

- Cattle cars which hold all of the beef, poultry, fish and other resources in this mighty country.

- Grain cars representing all of the agricultural and dairy products produced.

- Passenger cars that represent all of the different ways we can produce to move people domestically, internationally and interplanetarily.

- Tubular container cars that hold all the liquid commodities that need to be transported.

I hope you get the visual idea about the scale of this train we call the US economy and the diversity contained therein.

This train is pulled buy 12 huge engines, one engine for each Federal Open Market Committee (FOMC) member. The FOMC is comprised of the Board of Governors of the Federal Reserve System, the president of the New York Federal Reserve Bank and four rotating Federal Reserve Bank presidents. The engines are all synced together and are controlled by the engineer (The chairman of the Federal Reserve Open Market Committee). The throttle the engineer uses adjusts the FED funds interest rate; more throttle and interest rates rise, less throttle and interest rates lower.

This train travels on railroad tracks which are affected by the different financial events and factors influencing the United States economy. Over time the train encounters different terrain and landscapes, this is mainly a factor of where we are in the current business cycle. Sometimes this terrain is familiar and the engineer will know exactly what throttle setting to use on the locomotive engines to keep the train running at a steady speed. At other times the terrain is new and unmapped, in this case the engineer will need to be cautious if an adjustment to the engines is made.

It is the primary job of the Engineer to:

1. keep the train on the tracks

2. keep the train moving forward

3. keep the train at a fairly consistent speed no matter what the terrain of the economy is.

This isn't the easiest of jobs because the forward vision of the engineer is impaired. He just doesn't have a clear view of what the terrain far in the distance looks like or even what lies around the next bend in the railroad tracks. This train isn't always in the plain states; it travels the entire country and needs to deal with the varying terrain that this country is made of. The engineer does have very good side and rear vision to give him a reference as to where he may be on the tracks and how fast the train is moving.

The engineer has other resources available other than just looking out of the engine's windows to help him decide what the landscape should look like ahead of him. Experience is the first and most important in my opinion. He has studied the parts of the train and how all the parts function together. The engineer has also been plotting the course of the train tracks for many years. Most of the time he has a pretty good idea where his train is located, like the long stretches of the plain states where he can see no change in terrain for miles. Sometimes the scenery looks familiar, but the train may be on a different track than the last time it was in this area. This new track may require a slightly different adjustment to keep the train moving at a consistent speed. Other times the train is on uncharted tracks and the engineer is uncertain what the terrain is going to be like around the bend ahead. The engineer can only make a best guess as to what adjustments to the engine may be needed. Once around the corner and the engineer's vision of what awaits ahead improves, he can then select the best setting for the engines with more certainty.

The engineer isn't the only person onboard that has input into the throttle setting decisions. Each of the 11 other engines has it own engineer; they are the members of the FOMC, who also have the job of looking outside and giving input to the engineer in the first car. There are two-way radios onboard the engines which the 12 engineers can use to call out on for opinions from other resources. I'm sure these radios are constantly ringing off the hook with incoming calls from others (media, politicians and academia) who want to influence or have some say in how the engines are being run.

The engineer has to be looking and thinking very far ahead to make adjustments to the speed of the train before it arrives at a change in terrain. This is because of the huge number of freight cars and the weight being pulled. The momentum of the train means that time is needed for any change the engineer makes to take effect on the entire train. The engineer has to make subtle changes to the throttle otherwise it could spell disaster.

If the engineer looks down the railroad tracks as far as he can see and considers all of the available information, he may decide that there is an increasing elevation change (improving economy, increasing inflation) in front of the train. The engineer must also decide if the grade of the incline will require a change in the throttle setting of the engines. Remember, it's the 12 engineers' job to keep the train on the tracks and moving at a constant optimal speed. Will the engineer need to apply more power to the engines (raise interest rates to keep inflation from becoming an economic problem) to keep the train moving at a consistence speed? He must decide when to apply the power (raise interest rates) and by how much (percentage increase of FED Funds interest rate). Too much power applied at one time and the wheels driving the locomotive will lose their grip on the railroad tracks and start to spin, causing the train to slow down instead of speeding up. Once the driving wheels finally regain traction on the railroad tracks the locomotive could lurch forward, sending shock waves throughout the length of the train with the possibility of derailing all or part of the train (recession or depression). If too little power is applied, then the train (economy) will slow down as it is climbing the upward-sloping terrain. This may require a much stronger increase in power in the near future to catch up to the optimum speed.

On the other hand, if the engineer senses or sees a downward elevation change of terrain ahead on the railroad tracks (downturn in the economy), he will need to ease off the power to the engines (lower interest rates) to keep the train (economy) moving at a consistent optimal speed. If the engineer pulls back too hard on the power, the train will slow down too rapidly. In the extreme this change of momentum could possibly derail the whole train. It would take a lot of work to get the train back onto the tracks and moving forward at the optimal speed again. If too little power is removed, the train will continue to pick up speed. The power will need to be lowered even more to compensate for the extra speed. Remember, it is the goal of the engineers to keep this train moving at a constant optimal speed, no matter what terrain the train is traveling on.

Why do I give you a visual image to think about the economy as varying terrain? It's because located somewhere on this enormously long train is your personal liquid investment container car and also your personal freight car. Your personal things, your family, and maybe your business are being held in one or more of the different freight cars of this train we call the US economy. Your portfolio is affected by all the changes in the economic landscape and by the changes the engineer makes to the locomotive's throttles. You affect the train by your productivity to the economy, your earnings, your spending, your savings and your investing. This makes your car heavier the larger your portfolio gets, or lighter, this adds another factor that the engineers must take into consideration when making the throttle changes to the engines.

It's time to focus on your personal liquid investment railcar and the dynamic process of how to adjust your portfolio's asset allocation to meet the many different economic landscapes of the US economy. Like the train in this example your investments in your portfolio are affected by the three different environments: Rising interest rates, lowering interest rates, and steady interest rates as set by the Federal Open Market Committee. Your portfolio's asset allocation should key in on these interest rate (throttle) changes.

How much of an adjustment is needed in your portfolio is decided by many other factors such as: how long before you will retire, when you will need the money from your portfolio, the value of your investment portfolio, your experience with investing, and your overall risk tolerance. The younger you are, and more risk you should and can take. This taking more risk translates into more price volatility of your investments and the value of your portfolio. More risk means higher portfolio value highs and lower portfolio values lows over time, but ultimately a higher-priced portfolio at retirement. Before retirement your portfolio should be transitioned to remove much of the risk of price volatility. You do not want high price volatility in your portfolio beyond retirement age.

As you enter into the workforce you should immediately start saving for your emergency fund (equal to six months' income) and for your retirement. This is normally started with a savings account for the emergency fund and an employer-sponsored retirement account or ROTH IRA for the retirement account. The emergency fund may be called upon at any time so you need to keep the funds invested in a very stable liquid investment instrument, like a money market fund. You don't have the luxury of time to wait for your investments that may have gone down in your emergency fund to go back up. I like to open a special dedicated emergency fund money market or savings account. Every time I have co-mingled my emergency fund with my other personal savings, I tend to spend some or all of emergency fund. This takes financial discipline to both save for an emergency and to watch month over month as this money just sits there. Trust me, if you ever need the money in your emergency fund, you'll be so thankful the money is there.

I've used my emergency fund many times in my life and for all the right reasons. I now call my emergency fund my 'Freedom Fund'. My emergency fund gave me the freedom to change my life, freedom to leave a bad job, freedom to write this book and the freedom to be able to do what I want in life. It also gives me freedom from worrying about what will happen if I get seriously sick or injured. The emergency fund is not a down payment for a house fund or car repair fund, it's not a vacation fund or breast implants fund. It is an Emergency/Freedom fund! Please remember that!

Saving is boring. The only way I found a fun way to save was when I started racing cars. I know, that sounds totally insane, doesn't it? But I made a deal with myself. For every two dollars I saved in my retirement account, I could spend one guiltless dollar on racing cars. I found several new ways to save money over the next few years. I went through four different racecars and won several racing championships. I would say I was successful at both endeavors.

The soft asset investments in my universe are very liquid. This means that you could sell the investments and withdraw the money quickly without incurring significant losses or charges because you sold. Savings account, money market accounts and regularly traded stocks and bonds are liquid. As long as the bank or stock markets are open, you can ask for a withdrawal or sell your stock at the current stated price. I believe that an investor's first million dollars of investments should be liquid. We will use a liquid container railcar to hold your first million dollars worth of investments. As your investments grow you will add some illiquid assets like a house, car or even a business that will require a freight railcar be added to the train. This will be a square freight railcar with doors in the center of each side. This should give you an idea now how the length of the train can grow and grow and grow...

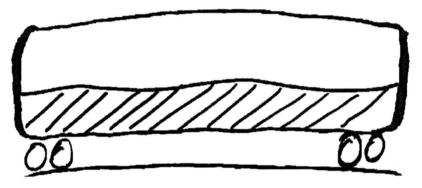

When you start out in life you have little or no investments, so your liquid investment container car is pretty empty. As you grow and your wealth increases so should the amount of liquid held inside of your liquid investment container car. The goal is to fill up this liquid investment car as full as possible before you retire so that when you retire you don't have to work anymore. I figure that the first liquid investment container car will top out at about one million dollars. If you exceed one million dollars of investments, great! It's time to add your second investment container car! Your investment options for the second car are much greater than the first.

I use the one-million-dollar amount for the maximum amount of your first liquid investment container car. I believe you can invest in plain vanilla investments such as stocks and bonds until you reach that amount. It is around the point of having one million dollars of investable assets that you should have your personal advisory team assembled: an investment advisor, insurance advisor, estate-planning advisor, tax advisor and legal advisor. You may at the one-million-dollar mark consider alternative investments which I describe as options, futures, forwards, foreign exchange, hedging strategies, venture capital, hedge funds, derivatives, portfolio insurance, commodity exposure and any other strategies that require an expert to administer. Remember that these investments should be allocated to your second investment container car. Any profits in the primary plain vanilla investment car can be transferred over to the secondary investment car. Your second investment container car will hold up to five million dollars of investments. If you manage to fill this car up, awesome! Now you really need to start handing off some of your personal tasks to the advisory team you should have assembled. If you haven't done that by now, DO IT!

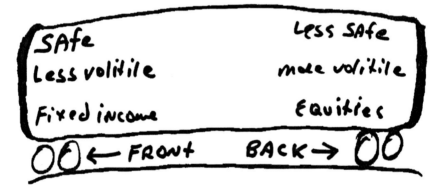

It's time look at the inside of your first liquid investment container car and see how I have laid it out. The front of the investment container is for the more secure, less price-volatile investments: fixed income and very high dividend paying equities that act like fixed income. As you move to the rear, the investment transitions from less volatile to more volatile: domestic large-cap equities, then mid-cap, small-cap and international equities.

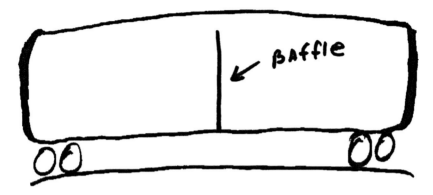

Here's the hard part. Added somewhere inside the container car is a baffle. This baffle will separate the growth area of the container car from the income area. This baffle is set by you to account for your personal age, risk tolerance, and investing experience. This baffle is not welded inside the liquid container so you can move it around as your age, risk tolerance, assets and experience change. The baffle also has openings in it so your investment capital can flow from one end of your liquid investment container car to the other.

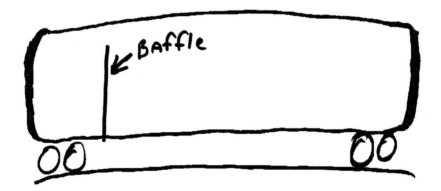

The younger you are, the closer your baffle should be to the front of the investment container car and most of your assets in growth, price-volatile investments.

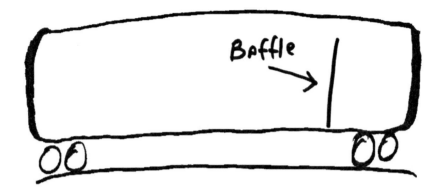

As you get closer to retirement age, your accumulated assets will need to be protected and therefore the baffle will move to the rear of the car. In front of the baffle in the container car is the amount of liquid inside the car allocated to safer income investments. Behind the baffle, to the back of the car, is the amount of liquid inside the car allocated to growth, price-volatile investments.

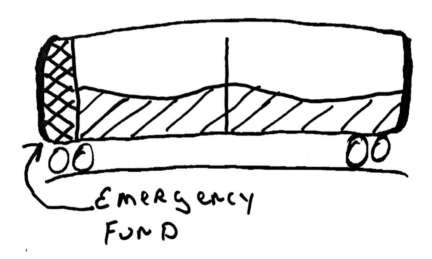

There are also a few permanent chambers that you will need in this car. They are for specific purposes and always need to be kept filled. The first chamber you need to fill will contain the

Emergency/Freedom fund money. You can have another chamber for the down payment for a car or house, vacation or even breast implants. They are always at the front of the car and always hold either money market or cash. You do not want to invest this cash and put the principal at risk in growth, price-volatile investments.

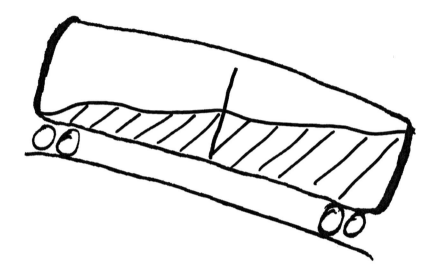

An improving and growing US economy is signified by an increase in elevation on the railroad tracks. The Federal Open Market Committee (FOMC) will be concerned about inflation and will soon be raising interest rates. Your container car is now higher in the front than in the back. Inside your investment container car gravity starts to affect the investment liquid. The liquid moves through the baffle, safer income investment dollars flow from the front of the liquid investment container car to growth investment in the rear. This flow adds dollars to the equity or growth portion from the income portion until the liquid investments level out. If the engineer has done his job properly, he will have raised interest rates just before getting to the rise in elevation. You will need to watch the financial news and anticipate the interest rate changes by the FOMC. You need only be concerned about the changes from an increasing interest rate to a decreasing rate or vice versa.

When the economy is not performing well, the train is declining and the investment liquid flows through the baffle to the front or to the income portion of your investment car from the growth portion. As the investment fluid levels out, you can see that more fluid is in the income portion and less in the growth portion. You should have adjusted you asset allocation before or as soon as the FOMC lowered interest rates. If you didn't, now is the time to sell some growth portion and buy some income portion. The level time on the tracks is the time to make your asset allocation portfolio changes.

When the railroad tracks are level, signified by stable interest rates, the economy is either at the top of a growth economic period or at the bottom of a weak economic period. You will need to be planning how you will be transitioning your portfolio asset allocation to take into account the upcoming change of direction the Federal Open Market Committee will make on interest rates. This level track scenario may be a fairly short period of time at the top of an economic cycle and usually a longer period of time at the bottom of an economic cycle. Wait until most experts all agree that interest rates will change and take note of what direction they will go. If you are concerned about making the wrong changes, wait until the FOMC changes the direction of interest rates to adjust your portfolio.

My tactical asset allocation model is pre-emptive in nature. For the best results you don't want to wait until the Federal Open Market Committee changes the direction of interest rates. If you follow mainstream news, you will have a good idea when the FOMC is about to change the rates. The most important thing to do is to make some type of adjustment to your asset allocation whenever the FOMC changes the direction of interest rates. If you can't do this for whatever reason, please, get your investments managed by someone who can. I can't tell you how many billions of dollars were lost from the top of the market in 1999 to the bottom in 2003 because investors couldn't make an asset allocation change or the sale decision. Most people can't do this, so you're in good company. That is why money management for individuals has really taken off in the past ten years. By that I mean balanced, age-specific mutual funds and investment professionals managing a person's investment account like a balanced mutual fund.

The amount of education and information needed to manage a well-allocated investment portfolio typically far exceeds the amount of time available to the average investor. That information needs to be continuously maintained in order to successfully manage a well-allocated investment portfolio. Another reason is that the professional money manager has no emotional connection to the money they are managing except to make your portfolio grow. In my opinion this allows money managers to make better hard investment decisions. This is called 'one degree of separation'. You set the parameters on how you want your money invested and the money managers do their best to invest your money the way you specify.

As you should have noticed, the baffle in you investment car acts as a moveable marker or guidepost. It usually helps decide what percentage of investment you should be close to as the economy changes. I keep a large bottle of water around with blue food coloring in it so that I can demonstrate this principle. My baffle is just a line drawn around the bottle with a magic marker. This doesn't have to be complicated to work.

The hard unending part of my model is figuring out where

you place the baffle for your portfolio. The younger and more risk tolerant you are, the closer to the front you should place your baffle. The older you get the closer to the rear your baffle should move. Accumulating more assets will help to determine these points and insulate you from wrong decisions. If you have to make a mistake, always make it on the side of more quality and less volatility. Remember that these points are guidelines to your asset allocation. This is a fluid model; you can always adjust the points as long as you realize that this will have a direct result in the risk/return of the portfolio.

Chapter 4

APPLYING MY ASSET ALLOCATION MODEL TO YOUR SPECIFIC NEEDS

Before you can get to the specifics of your financial action plan you need to outline a few 'BIG PICTURE' objectives:

- What are your investment goals?

- How am I going to save enough to reach my financial goals?

- What kind of investor are you?

- What asset classes should you invest in?

- Will you use individual stocks/bonds or pooled investments like mutual funds and ETFs?

- What percentage of your assets should be allocated to the three major asset classes?

- What is the process to 'rebalance' or bring your portfolio back to your specific asset allocation?

My job is to work for people who have decided that it is important for them to save money for a specific goal. I do my job by taking the factors listed above and putting them into practice. Why do you think most professional investment advisors, the really good ones, require a minimum account size of over $250,000 before they will talk to you? It's very simple. Someone who can save that amount of money has decided that their personal finances are very important to them. These savers have decided that they want to retire in style and will commit the time, energy and their financial resources to seeing it to the very end. It is so much easier to work with these successful savers because we are all working towards the same goal, their financial well-being.

I used the verb 'save' not 'inherit' or 'win' a big lawsuit. Instant wealth has no history or hard work behind it. There is no tangible connection to this quick, easy money, and it is usually pissed away as quickly as it was received. I've seen it happen almost every time I've dealt with instant wealth. Ever wonder why so many lottery winners are poor just a few years after 'Hitting it Big'? There is no connection to the money they won.

It is not my job to show you how to save and reduce your debt. I can say with some certainty that 80% of you reading this book haven't come close to saving enough for your retirement. I can also say with certainty that you don't learn from your own investment mistakes. This has a direct influence on most do-it-yourself investors investing either far too aggressively or far too conservatively. I have spent a lot of my personal time helping people who have convinced me they are saving because retirement is important to them but didn't have the minimum amount to be accepted at the firm I worked for. I charge them nothing for my time, resources and energy.

WHAT ARE YOUR INVESTMENT GOALS?

Do you have any? Have you ever even thought about this question? It is so easy to convince yourself that you'll have plenty of money to retire on, even though you have saved next to nothing. Most people have convinced themselves that somehow, somewhere they will come across enough money to live comfortably throughout their retirement years. That's a fairy tale.

A person without any goals has no way of measuring where they are along any journey. Goals are:

- Measurable, specific values.

- Reviewed at specific points in time to compare where you are now with where you want to be.

'I want to be rich' is not measurable. 'I want $1,000,000 at age 55' is measurable and is set to a particular date; this is a valid goal unless you aged 54, earning $50,000 a year and have $2,000 in the bank. A person without financial goals can't prepare for retirement in any worthwhile way. A person who can't save can't prepare for retirement. You will live hand-to-mouth/paycheck-to-paycheck for the rest of your life. If you plan on retiring after 2020 don't count on the Social Security program, it won't be there. It was a program put into place during the great depression of the 1930's. It was not meant to last this long. Demographics and retiring baby-boomers will suck that program dry. POOF it's gone! No more money, back to work at age 70, 80, or 90!

The point is to start saving and save twice what you think you will need. You will live longer than you think! If you can't save any sum of money, this book is useless to you. Like I said earlier, saving for anything is boring. I make saving important to me because I see so many people who will have never be able to retire. Just look at the bag boys at the grocery store. They are no longer boys; they are retirees who didn't save enough during their life to retire on. They will be working for the rest of their lives.

WHAT KIND OF INVESTOR ARE YOU?

Now let's take a look at how I figure out what kind of investor you are. I start with how many years you have until you retire.

THE AGE YOU PLAN TO RETIRE minus YOUR CURRENT AGE = _____

A number greater than ten years will automatically make you a **LONG-TERM INVESTOR**. Your portfolio should be geared for growth. Your baffle in the liquid container car will be closer to the front of the car. You need your retirement assets working hard for you now, growing so that one day you can eventually live off the income produced inside your portfolio. That doesn't mean an investment portfolio filled with every aggressive investment. It means you will have investments in your portfolio geared for growth, and yes, that does include bonds at times.

Growth investor liquid container car

If the number of years you have until you retire is between one and ten, you are a **TRANSITIONAL INVESTOR**. You will need to be thinking about transitioning your portfolio from a growth objective to an income and growth objective. You have ten years to make this transition so do it smart and use the different interest rate cycles to your greatest advantage. You have time to plan and make unrushed, smart financial decisions.

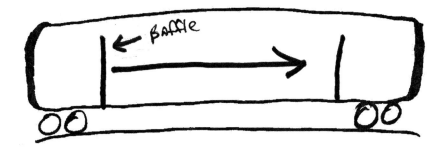

Transitional investor liquid container car

If the number of years you have until you retire is zero or negative, congratulations, you're retired! You will be referred to as an **INCOME AND GROWTH** investor. I hope you have saved enough to enjoy retirement. You will need to structure your portfolio to produce the extra income you will need while keeping a portion in the growth area to account for inflation, various changing personal needs and emergencies. If you haven't transitioned your portfolio, continue to read on. You may want to wait for the right interest rate environment to adjust your portfolio.

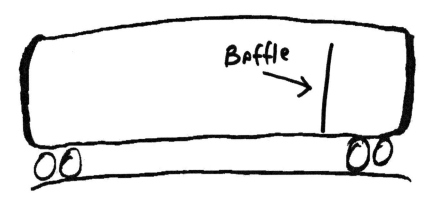

Income and growth liquid container car

HOW TO MEASURE YOUR RISK TOLERANCE

Another part of determining what kind of investor you are is getting a feel for your risk tolerance. My definition of risk is price volatility. The more risk an investment has, the more volatile the price movements will be on both the upside and downside. Some factors determining equity risk are:

- Market capitalization of the company, larger equals less risk.

- How much debt the company has, smaller equals less risk.

- Depth and breadth of product line, more equals less risk.

- Management characteristics.

- Earning forecasts have a big impact on the present value of that investment.

Risks for bonds are a little easier because of their mathematical nature. Most bonds are tracked by Moody's or Standard and Poors or other credit rating agencies. So upfront you have an independent assessment of credit quality. The lower quality the rating on the bond, the higher the risk/price volatility of the bond. Bonds' other main risk is the changing of interest rates. The longer the maturity date, the more volatile the price will be when interest rates change. Bonds may have specific hard assets attached to them as collateral making them less risky. Municipal bonds can be insured by an agency, basically guaranteeing all interest payments and principal at maturity; this makes the bond less risky.

If you can mathematically describe the last two paragraphs on risk, then you could win a Nobel Prize. There are thousand of books written on this subject of risk, but it still hasn't been totally defined. It is written and taught so much because understanding risk is very important. I know far more than I want to know about this subject, yet it's still not enough. This knowledge helps define the various investment markets, and the various individual investments and investors. It's one of the tools that guide me in defining what my client's asset allocation should be, but it is hard to explain. It is more art than science; experience and motivation are very important.

Below is my 'risk meter'.

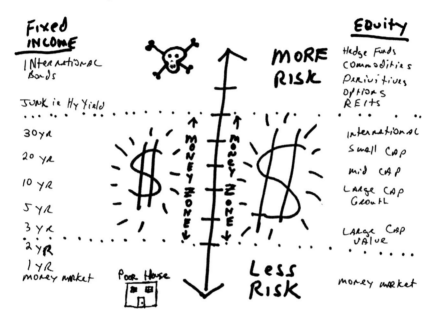

Accepting more risk in your portfolio usually translates into higher price volatility for your portfolio. Higher risk should make the amount of time before you can comfortably retire shorter and the amount you actually have to deposit into your retirement account less.

The less risk you can accept, the more money you will need to deposit into your retirement account and the longer time it will take before you can retire.

The smart investor will focus on a compromise in the center of the risk meter; I call this the 'Money Zone', and then adjust their asset allocation to the current market conditions. The smart money is made in moderation.

BIG PICTURE CONCEPT: If you invest only in high-risk investments, there could be dire consequences, like losing all of your money. If you don't accept some level of risk, you may fail to get a high enough return on your investments and end up working your whole life. Invest your first million dollars of investments in the 'Money Zone'.

WHAT ASSET CLASSES SHOULD YOU INVEST IN?

I'm a firm believer that your first million dollars of investments should be in 'Plain Vanilla' investments: stocks, bonds and money market. There are many different investments vehicles available for these three classes of investments: individual securities, Exchange Traded Funds (ETF), open and closed-end mutual funds and individual money managers. The more money you have to invest the more options available to invest in.

WHAT PERCENTAGE OF YOUR ASSETS SHOULD BE ALLOCATED TO THE THREE MAJOR ASSET CLASSES?

LONG-TERM INVESTOR

If you have ten or more years until retirement, my model has labeled you a 'Long-Term Investor'. You need to be thinking 'long-term growth' in your investment strategies. You have time to save and make your money work for you. You should expect to see several business cycles before you retire, so start planning now for them.

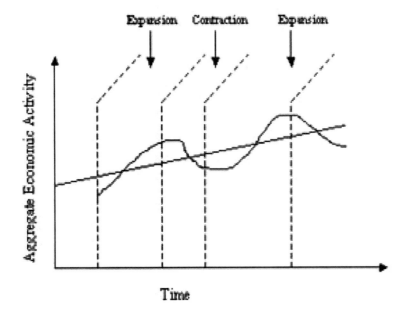

Graph copied from External Factors – The Economy lesson on

http://www.learnthings.co.uk/cima-mc/lesson3/business_cycle__ 11236.jpg

Don't be surprised to see a few recessions in your life and maybe even a depression. On the plus side you should see plenty of good years for the economy and stock markets. Downturns in the market are traditionally shorter but much more severe than the upward movements of the markets. Don't get overly worried, but be smart about where you allocate your assets and how you change your asset allocation to adjust for the different market climates. Position your investment dollars to make money in all business cycles.

I would recommend that if you have little or no experience in investing start low-risk (conservatively) and work your way up the risk meter. As you become more experienced and comfortable with investing, you can move into more risky, price-volatile and aggressive asset allocation. Don't ever make any huge reactive asset allocation change to your portfolio; investing is a subtle art form. Once you make an asset allocation or investment change, you will need to give that change time to have an effect, like six months or so. You are a LONG-TERM INVESTOR, so start thinking long-term.

Watch your monthly statements closely to see if one or two investments have performed above or below the rest. If you have too much in one asset class, you may need to rebalance your portfolio to bring it back to your ideal mix. I've read several studies that suggest that more rebalancing produces better returns. A $100,000-portfolio will need more rebalancing than a $10,000 one. They both need the same attention, just different levels of action.

The following are some general asset allocation guidelines I use as an investment professional for the long-term investor. Review, then determine what your asset allocation should be. Investing is a very personal experience. Take the time to personalize your asset allocation and learn how you manage the financial people in your life.

Guidelines for the long-term Investor in a rising interest rate environment:

	CONSERVATIVE INVESTOR	AGGRESSIVE INVESTOR
Growth	70%	100%
Fixed income/cash	30%	0%

CONSERVATIVE

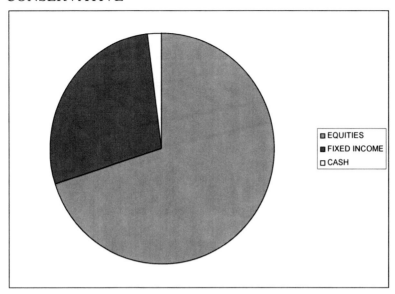

AGGRESSIVE

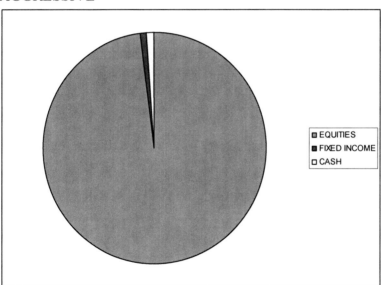

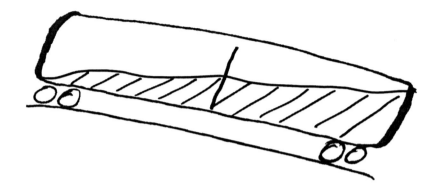

Notice the very high allocation in the equity asset class. Equity traditionally does better in a rising interest rate environment. The FOMC is raising rates to keep inflation in check. Inflation is usually caused by high demand of inputs used to create a finished product: raw materials, energy and labor are the big inputs. So inflation is a pretty good determinant of a strong business environment.

With rising interest rates the rails that our liquid container car is on slope upwards. Your liquid assets should flow to the back of your liquid container car, where your equity investments are.

Guidelines for the long-term investor in a decreasing interest rate environment:

	CONSERVATIVE INVESTOR	AGGRESSIVE INVESTOR
Growth	35%	50%
Fixed income/cash	65%	50%

CONSERVATIVE

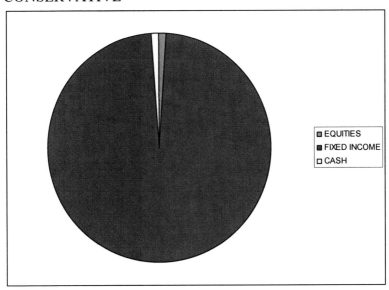

AGGRESSIVE

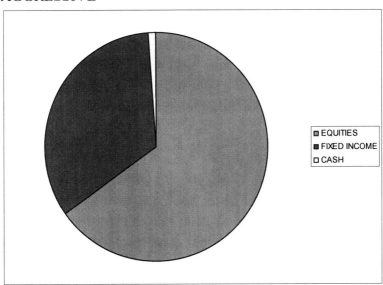

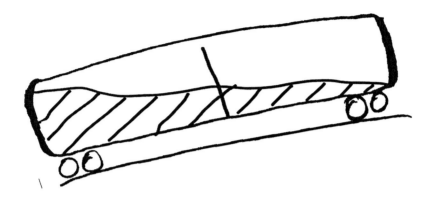

Why the big difference in the asset allocation between rising and lowering interest rates for the long-term investor in growth and fixed-income asset allocation?

As a long-term investor with more than ten years to retirement, you can use any and all investment vehicles in your portfolio. From ultra-safe short-term US Treasury Bills to high-risk emerging market equities. Maybe not all at one time, but you can certainly use the entire galaxy of investment vehicles available. How you allocate your equity allocation is up to the economy, your personal risk tolerance and your personal investment style.

Keep in mind that if you put all your money into an emerging markets mutual fund, you are too concentrated in one position or asset class, this could cause your portfolio to collapse in a sudden market change. A good rule of thumb would be for every risky investment dollar you have twice that much in a much less risky equity category like large-cap growth. That equates to: **at any point in time will you have no more than a third of your portfolio in very high-risk investments**.

If you are comfortable with all of your assets in the stock market, then have them there. Comfortable defined as being able to 'sleep at night' not worried at the end of each day where the stock market ended up. You have to realize that the stock market is price volatile. As a long-term investor you have the time to make that volatility work for you. Money and wealth is supposed to enhance your life, not make you lose sleep or constantly worry. You do need to worry about saving enough and living within your means to be able to save enough for retirement. Also keep in mind that bonds do outperform stocks on occasion.

Since you have no real need of income at this point in your life, your bond investment will need to be skewed to bond investments that have capital appreciation as the main focus. **Wait! You mean people can invest in bonds and make capital gains? YES!** When you get to the chapter on making money with bonds, you will mainly want to focus on investing in zero-coupon, long-maturity bonds in a lowering interest rate environment. Use coupon short-term bonds, three-year or less, in a rising interest rate environment. Make sure you read about the other bonds, they may make more sense to you and you'll need to know about investing in all types of bonds.

I have spent a lot of brain compute time trying to figure out how much equity should go to fixed income during a lowering interest rate environment. I have crunched lots of numbers, built a hefty spreadsheet taking all kinds of variables into account; it was a bear importing in all the variables. These models created good asset allocation models, but they were not something the average investor could manage.

Instead of the process of getting the results, I started to look at the results. Surprisingly the answer was pretty simple. In a lowering interest rate environment, move 50% of you equity to fixed income. The portfolio with 100% equity in a rising interest rate environment has 50% equity and 50% fixed income in a decreasing interest rate environment. The portfolio with 70% equity in a rising interest rate environment has 35% equity and 65% fixed income in a decreasing interest rate environment.

TRANSITIONAL INVESTOR

If you have ten or fewer years until retirement, my model has labeled you a 'Transitional Investor'. You need to be thinking about transitioning your growth portfolio to an income-based portfolio with some growth. The really big question that you need to ask yourself right now is: "Have I saved enough to cover all of my needs until I die?" You only have ten years left to finish saving for retirement or to pick what job you want to do until you die.

You will need to transition your portfolio before you retire. This transition doesn't need to happen all at once or every year. You'll need to use changes in the market to take advantage of adjusting your portfolio. Always keep in mind that you have ten years to make this transformation, be smart about the changes to your asset allocation.

If you have three years until retirement and the FOMC has started lowering interest rates, you may want to overweight the fixed income area or even look at the 'income and growth' model for your asset allocation. If interest rates are rising, then you may want to stay overweight allocated on equities for a while before making the adjustment. Just don't wait until your retirement party to start planning the transition of your investment portfolio.

Guidelines for the transitional investor in a increasing interest rate environment:

	CONSERVATIVE INVESTOR	AGGRESSIVE INVESTOR
Equity	50%	70%
Fixed income/cash	50%	30%

CONSERVATIVE

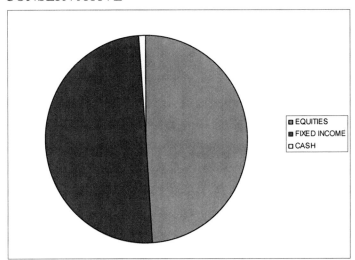

AGGRESSIVE

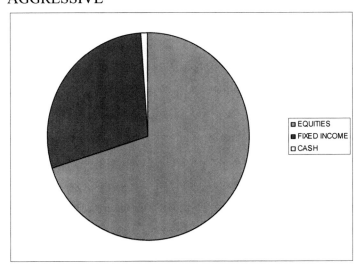

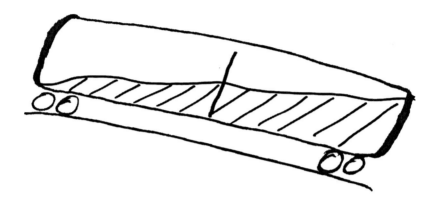

Guidelines for the transitional investor in a decreasing interest rate environment:

	CONSERVATIVE INVESTOR	AGGRESSIVE INVESTOR
Equity	25%	35%
Fixed income and money market	75%	65%

CONSERVATIVE

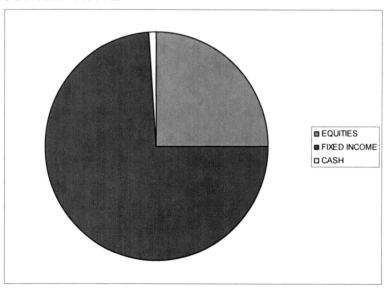

AGGRESSIVE

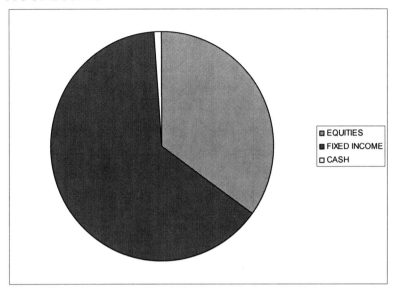

EQUITIES
FIXED INCOME
CASH

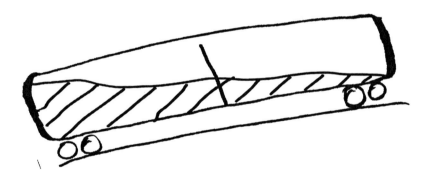

Over the next few years and before you retire, you should be eliminating the very risky investments in your portfolio. You may not have the time to recover from the possible catastrophic losses you could incur in this very price-volatile investment sector. Your percentage of more price-stable investments should be increasing as you see advantages in the market. You will need to start looking at bonds that pay a coupon and are over ten years to maturity. In the making money on bonds chapter, focus on coupon bonds and investing in them. You can still use zero-coupon bonds for capital appreciation. Also, don't load up on long-term bonds in a low interest rate environment.

INCOME AND GROWTH INVESTOR

You are retired or almost there. I don't care who you are, how much money you have saved or how aggressive of an investor you are, it's time to get a new perspective on investing. It is time to lock in some capital gains in your portfolio and prepare to start taking income out. To do this you will need to have income-producing investments. Now I hope you noticed that I didn't say 'fixed income'. You can own equities that generate lots of income, but the safest way is with fixed-income debt instruments.

Owning bonds and equities from large, solid companies with very little speculation should be your first concern. Now is not the time to be a high-risk investor. The downside of high-risk investing at this time in your life could cause you to lose enough of the value of your portfolio that you **HAVE TO** come out of retirement and work for the rest of your life. Remember all those retired 'Dot com'ers' who retired until their stocks crashed between 2000 and 2004. They **HAD TO** go back to work! Live within your income and upgrade your income-producing investments on your terms. Watch the maturities, credit rating and call features on your long-term bonds.

Guidelines for the income and growth investor in an increasing interest rate environment:

	CONSERVATIVE INVESTOR	AGGRESSIVE INVESTOR
Equity	20%	30%
Fixed income and money market	80%	70%

CONSERVATIVE

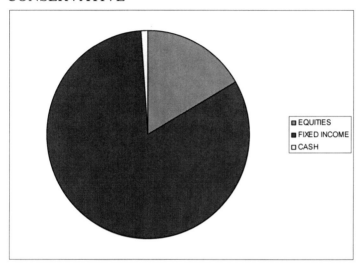

AGGRESSIVE

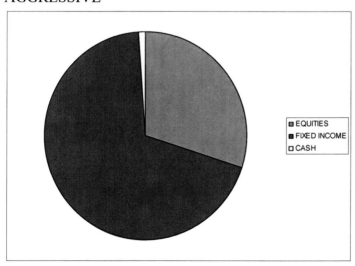

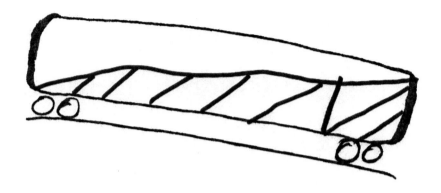

Guidelines for the income and growth investor in a decreasing interest rate environment:

	CONSERVATIVE INVESTOR	AGGRESSIVE INVESTOR
Equity	15%	20%
Fixed income and money market	85%	80%

CONSERVATIVE

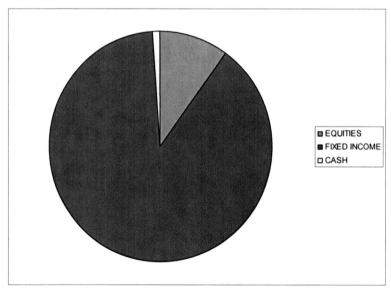

AGGRESSIVE

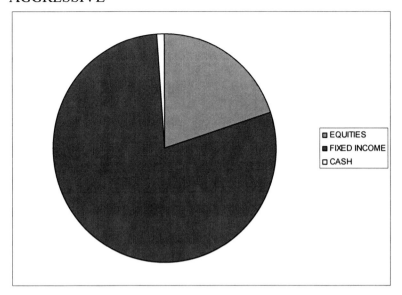

EQUITIES
FIXED INCOME
CASH

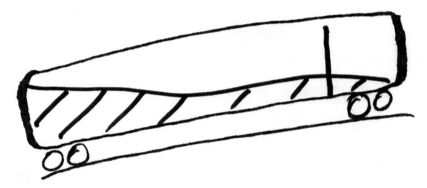

You should have noticed that for the conservative investor I didn't reduce the equity position by 50%. This is because no matter what type of investor you are, you need 15% in equities at all times.

THE 2% FUN FACTOR

The 2% fun factor? Yes, investing is a serious business, that doesn't mean that it has to be boring. It's OK to set aside some investment funds, no more than 2%, to play with. I define 'play' as investing in a company whose product or service you really like. My current play investment is a public company that looks for sunken treasure ships. Will they find any? I don't know, but I really like the idea of being the owner of a treasure-hunting company. It makes me smile and laugh owning this company. I went so far as to contact the CEO while I was writing this book to ask if I could serve as a hand on their boat or dive for treasure with them. They were at that time salvaging yachts that sunk in the Florida Keys by the hurricanes of 2005 to pay the treasure-hunting bills. I wanted to hunt for treasure, not perform salvage work for an insurance company, so I passed on that.

I know clients of mine who use their 2% fun-factor money to buy stock in the company they work for. Others like to own stock in the supermarket they shop at. Don't expect to make much money with this investment. I would consider myself lucky if I break even. I already have a very positive 'emotional' return from owning this treasure-hunting company. I also don't have close to 2% of my investment total tied up in this company.

If your 2% investment goes down in value, you don't get another 2%. Your portfolio will have to grow back to the value that you started at when you made your 2% fun-factor purchase, and then some. If your 2% investment grows and you sell for a profit, the funds must go back into your main portfolio. You can then put another 2% aside for another fun-factor investment. This is my way of making investing a little less stressful and more enjoyable. **Remember, ONLY 2% MAX!**

Chapter 5

TIME VALUE OF MONEY

Time value of money (TVM) is as much a statement as it is a financial concept. TVM states that if I give you $100 today, you will at some set date in the future pay me back that $100 plus some monetary value to compensate me for not having use of my money. When you have my $100, I can't use my $100, I can't invest my $100, I can't spend my $100 and I can't even hold my $100. I need to be compensated for missed opportunities while you have my $100. TVM is used to help place a monetary value on the time you have my money, or I have someone else's money.

Time value of money (TVM) is at the heart of finance. The average investor will never really understand the stock market until they learn TVM. It's the biggest, most important concept of finance, Wall Street, business and money. Once understood, TVM will give you a greater insight into not only how Wall Street values money, but also banks and business. TVM is a universal concept applied to money all over the world. TVM works the same in every language, currency and marketplace.

TVM will answer many finance questions in your lives. TVM is used to break down complex financial problems in the business world. The boards of directors for most large companies don't have the time to read a several-hundred-page project report for a new proposed multimillion-dollar factory.

The board of directors typically read the one page executive summary. They then look at the predicted cash flows of the project on a time line. If the time line for this project in the executive summary shows a positive cash flow, which means that this project, at least on paper, should be a profitable venture. The project may get the go-ahead at this review. The time line also shows the interest rate on the money borrowed or the money lent out along with an overall rate of return for the project. Typically projects with the greater rates of return are approved over projects with lower rates of return.

TIME LINES

Time lines are an excellent visual representation showing all cash flows, interest rates, time horizons and time units for one particular transaction.

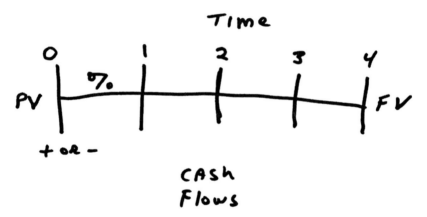

The time line can move from left to right to solve for a Future Value (FV), or it can move from right to left to solve for Present Value (PV).

Time units will be marked on the top of the time line. Time units can be in years, months or semiannually, but time must be consistent through the entire time line. You can't start with monthly payments and then halfway through change to annual payments. That scenario would require two time lines, one for the time when monthly payments are made and another timeline for when annual payments are made. Time lines are custom tailored to whatever the cash flows being plotted are.

Along with time, the interest rate applied in this time line is listed in the first upper left time segment above the main line. The interest rate must be consistent through the entire time line. A fixed rate mortgage can be plotted on one time line. An adjustable rate mortgage can't be plotted on one time line because you don't know what interest rate you will be paying in the future when the interest rate adjusts.

Cash flows appear on the bottom, below the time line. At the bottom left end we see the opening transactions, either the loaning or borrowing of your money. I like to think of negative cash flow when I have to take money out of my pocket. For the bond buyer an initial negative cash flow would indicate that I have loaned money out, money coming out of my pockets.

I like to think of a positive cash flow as money coming into my pocket. An initial positive cash flow would indicate that I have borrowed money; the money goes into my pocket. Then each predetermined payment date is a negative cash flow showing the interest and/or principal payment I have to make.

There are five basic pieces of information you need to know before constructing a time line. You will need to have four out of the five below pieces of information to solve a TVM question.

1. All starting cash flows, the amount you are borrowing, lending or investing. This is in today's dollar terms, Present Value (PV).

2. The number of payments that will occur at regularly scheduled times and how often they are paid: 10-year semi-annual payment, 48 monthly payments or 20 annual payments.

3. The stated interest rate that this time line will either pay or expects to earn.

4. The scheduled loan payment or expected inflows of cash amount.

5. All ending cash flows. Normally on a car or home loan this is zero, just the last payment closed the contract and time line. On an investment it will be the target price on a stock. On a building or machine it will be the salvage value.

SOLVING FOR FUTURE VALUE

Future Value (FV) tells us or predicts what an investment will be worth in the future. This means that we need to use all Present Value (PV) inputs into the formulas. The formula for FV is:

$$FV = PV(1+i)^n$$

FV= Future Value, this is what we are solving

PV= the Present Value of the investment

i = interest rate we are using in the problem 5%=.05 & 10%=.10

n = number of time units that we need to account for going forward

Nothing too scary here; a pretty simple formula without any fractions. We will now apply the Future Value formula to a real-world problem. You have $100 (PV= $100) and want to buy a three-year bond (n=3) that pays interest once a year at 5% (i=.05). How much money will you have at the end of the three years? You might think $115, but you haven't calculated the interest on the interest over the three years.

Now a big caveat with this formula is that it is assumed that all interest paid by the bond will be reinvested at the same interest rate as the bond. This in plain English means that interest rates will remain steady until the bond matures; I know that this is not a valid 'real-world' assumption, but let's get the basics down. First we draw a time line:

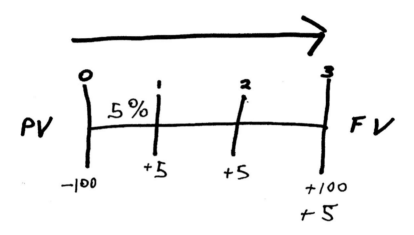

The time line moves from left to right because we wantt to know what the money will be worth in the future. We will take $100 out of our pocket at the start of this investment, that's why it has a negative sign in front of it. At the end of the first, second and third year, we will receive $5 interest ($100 x .05 = $5). At the end of the third year we will also receive back our original investment of $100. We will now solve the formula:

$$FV = PV(1+i)^n$$

PV=$100

i=.05

n=3

$$FV = \$100(1+.05)^3$$

$$FV = \$100(1.05)^3$$

$FV = \$100(1.1576)$ solve for the number inside the parentheses first

$FV = \$115.76$

NOTE: When using any type of calculator/computer to solve an equation, it is important to know that rounding is handled differently by each machine or computer program. Your answer to this problem may be + or – a small amount, but that's normal.

Here is a timeline that shows how the formula works. The initial investment of $100 is multiplied by 1.05 to equal $105. This is the amount of money you would have at the end of year 1. As a wise investor I took the $5 interest payment I received and put the money into a 5% saving account. In year 2 we get interest not only on the original $100 investment, but also on the extra $5 I put into the savings account. Inside the saving account the $5 has grown to $5.25. We add year 2's $5 interest and we now have $10.25 in the savings account. At the end of year 3 we get back our $100 plus $5 in interest. The saving account has grown to $10.76. The total cash we now have is $115.76.

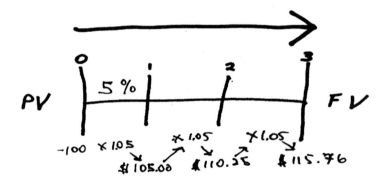

So you see by solving this equation you will receive back $115.76 and not 115.00. This timeline shows us that we get our $100, $15 in interest (3X$5) and also $.76 of interest on our interest (compound interest).

- If your investment of $100 was for 5 years, the compound interest on $100 in this example would be $2.63.

- If your investment of $100 was for 10 years, the compound interest on $100 in this example would be $62.88.

- If your investment of $100 was for 20 years, the compound interest on $100 in this example would be $165.32.

- If your investment of $100 was for 30 years, the compound interest on $100 in this example would be $332.19.

That's a big difference! Compound interest continually grows exponentially the longer the investment lasts.

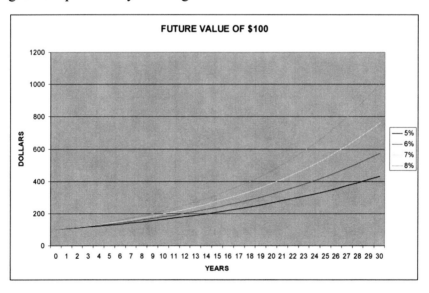

Above is a chart of $100 invested at different interest rates over 30 years. The top line is at 8% return ending at $1,000 and bottom line is 5%, the 30-year value is $432.19 ($100 initial investment and $332.19 interest). This chart shows us that at a higher return an investment will grow faster.

THE RULE OF 72

This rule tells you how quickly your investment will double in value. Take 72 and divide it by the rate of return of the investment. It would take nine years (72/8=9) for $100 to become $200 at 8%. You can see that in the above graph. Eight percent is the top line and intersects the $200 line in year 9. At 5% return it would take 14 years (72/5=14.2) for an investment to double. That can be seen above; the bottom line is 5% return, this line intersecting the $200 level in year 14. I use this Rule of 72 constantly as an easy way to compare investments and returns.

SOLVING FOR PRESENT VALUE

Present Value (PV) tells us what a value in the future is worth in today's dollars.

Formula

$$PV = FV_n \left(\frac{1}{1+i} \right)^n$$

PV = Present Value, what we are solving for

FV_n = Future Value, the value of an investment at **n** time units future time

i = interest rate we are using in the problem

n = number of time units in the future that we need to backtrack to present time

This formula should look a little familiar; it's the FV

formula with the PV/FV swapped and the interest rate inverted. I will use the same example we used to solve for FV, but in reverse to solve for PV. You have been told that an investment will be worth $115.76 (FV=$115.76) in three years (n=3) that pays interest once a year at 5% (i=.05).

Same assumption: all interest paid by the investment will be reinvested at the same interest rate as the bond.

First we draw a time line, notice that we are moving from right to left for PV:

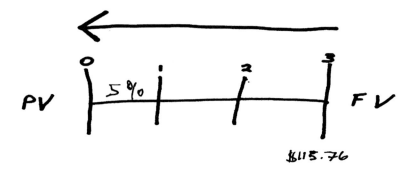

Now we solve for Present Value:

$$PV = FV_n \left(\frac{1}{1+i} \right)^n$$

$FV_n = \$115.76$

$i=.05$

$n=3$

$$PV = \$115.76 \left(\frac{1}{1+.05} \right)^3$$

$$PV = \$115.76\left(\frac{1}{1.05}\right)^3$$

$PV = \$115.76(.952381)^3$ solve for number inside parentheses

$PV = \$115.76(.863838)$

$PV = \$100$

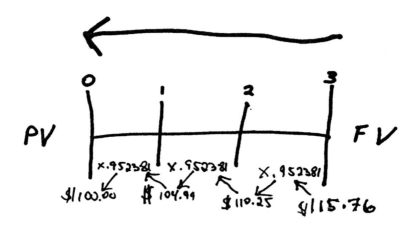

Notice the rounding difference at the one-year time point. It should be $105, but my calculator came up with $104.99. The answer to our question still came out correct at $100.

Here's a time line for the car purchase. Let's say your dream car cost $30,000. You have a car to trade in valued at $10,000. The loan amount will be for $20,000. The term of the loan is four years. Payments will be made monthly. The interest rate on the loan will be at 5.0%.

1. Starting cash flows trade in   -$10,000

      Loan   -$20,000

      Total out of pocket cost of car   -$30,000

At this point you have a car worth $30,000 and a loan for -$20,000

2. 48 monthly payments on the loan

3. Interest rate of 5%

4. This number we do not have and need to calculate. I will spare you the math and tell you it is $460.59. To come up with the answer is a trial and error method without a financial calculator, all the more reason to buy a Texas Instruments BA II PLUS or a comparable financial calculator. You may come up with a slightly different number due to rounding differences in the calculators. It should not be more than a few pennies.

5. Ending cash flow will be the final payment only. There is no other lump sum due at the end of a typical car or home loan.

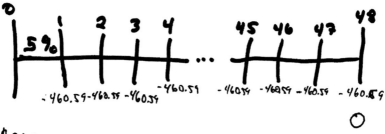

Cash flows are easy to visualize. Do you put the money in your pocket/purse or take it out? You will put $10,000 into your pocket/purse (positive) from your trade-in and you will put $20,000 (positive) into your pocket/purse from the bank loan. That means that you now have $30,000 cash in your pocket and a loan for $20,000. To take the car off the lot you have reach into your pocket and hand over the price of the car to the dealer, $30,000(negative cash flow). You now own a new car and a loan for $20,000. The bank will now receive 48 payments of

$460.59 (negative cash flows) over the next four years or 48 monthly payments in exchange for giving you the $20,000 today.

Understanding TVM helps us make better financial decisions on how we spend money. You want to get the best return/product for money spent, so you need to compare different products or services when you shop. You weigh the advantages and disadvantages of each purchase against your needs and wants. You can use TVM to help make those comparisons so you weigh apples to apples and oranges to oranges. Like in the car finance example, you can use TVM and see what your monthly payments are to save money and make more informed buying decisions. You could also start with the monthly payment you can afford, then do the math to see how much you can afford to finance for a car or a home.

Real-world investment use of TVM: You are looking at two stocks to buy today. Both will cost $100.00 to buy one share. Stock A is a smaller growth company that pays no dividend. Stock B is considered a mature company with slower growth but pays a once-a-year dividend of $2.00. You expect Stock A to grow at the market average of 12.5% over the next three years, and stock B to grow at 8% per year. An interest-bearing account will pay 5% over the next three years. You already have a fully diversified portfolio and the addition of either investment will not push your portfolio's asset allocation to one investment group or another, therefore there is no need for rebalancing. Which stock will make you more money? Let's start with the time lines.

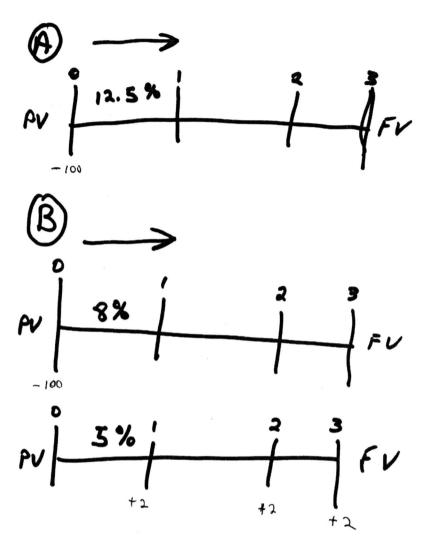

In this example we will solve for the future value (FV) because it just makes sense to value the project in ending dollars. We know all present value figures, but what we really want to know is the total value three years in the future. You will see that for stock B we have two different timeline lines, that's due to the two different interest rates we are applying to stock B. One timeline for rate of return for the price appreciation of the stock which is at 8%. The second timeline for the interest rate that is earned on the dividends, which is 5%.

STOCK A

$$FV = PV(1+i)^n$$

$$FV = 100(1+.125)^3$$

$$FV = 100(1.125)^3$$

$$FV = 100(1.423828)$$

$$FV = \$142.38$$

STOCK B

PRICE	FIRST DIVIDEND	SECOND DIVIDEND	THIRD DIVIDEND
$FV = PV(1+i)^n$	$FV = PV(1+i)^n$	$FV = PV(1+i)^n$	$FV = PV(1+i)^n$
$FV = 100(1+.08)^3$	$FV = 2(1+.05)^2$	$FV = 2(1+.05)^1$	$FV = 2(1+.05)^0$
$FV = 100(1.08)^3$	$FV = 2(1.05)^2$	$FV = 2(1.05)^1$	$FV = 2(1.05)^0$
$FV = 100\,(1.259712\,)$	$FV = 2(1.1025)$	$FV = 2(1.05)$	$FV = 2(1.00)$
$FV = \$125.97$	$FV = \$2.20$	$FV = \$2.05$	$FV = \$2.00$

$FV= \$125.97+\$2.20+\$2.05+\$2.00=130.22$

Stock A is worth $142.38 after three years and stock B with dividends accounted for is worth $132.20. Stock A would be the better investment in this example.

We can make timelines as complicated as any normal business transaction is. Think about all the financial time lines for building a new skyscraper, there would be thousands of them. Some time lines would begin years before the construction part of the project, architecture or design costs, acquiring the land where the project is to be built, getting the appropriate government approvals and permits. If you are building for the purpose of renting out most of the space, you will have time lines to project how much you will receive in rents for the space once built, occupancy rates, cost of borrowing money to complete the construction, cost of maintaining the building or any other of a number of factors that influence this type of rental space. Our time line for this project could be thirty to forty years long. Once all of the thousands of cash flows are determined or estimated, then a master financial time line for the project will be completed, cash flows are listed and interest rates that will be applied to both borrowed and received money are added. This huge time line is then simplified and presented to the board of directors for their proceed/cancel decision. There will be many proceed/cancel decisions made before ground is broken for the construction phase on a project of this size.

As you probably guessed, timelines can be used for more applications than just finance. I've seen some construction project time lines that were so big they had to be displayed on a wall, a very long wall. Every week of work on the project was plotted on this time line as a column, and every subcontractor's job to be preformed was displayed on its own row. Each subcontractor was brought in and shown their job responsibility and the time frame in which they had to complete their specific jobs. When a job was completed by a subcontractor that job would be highlighted. Green highlighter for on-time completion of a specific job, and red highlighter for late completion of a specific job. A black diagonal stripe was added if a worker was injured performing this job. Many other colors could be used to show any other performance or incident data on the massive timeline. No compromise, no excuses, everyone knew exactly what was required of them, when it needed to be done and how they were performing.

LAST REAL-WORLD TVM APPLICATION

Here is my favorite real-world example of how TVM has saved me lots of money. It's a well-known fact that when you buy a car at the dealership the salesperson who does the paperwork for the sale will get a part of the purchase price in the form of a commission. What most people don't know is that the person at that same dealership who arranges the loan for that same car is also working on commission. Oh, you thought that the dealership, out of the goodness of their heart, would allocate valuable resources hiring someone, training them and furnishing them a decent office so that you will get a car loan to buy their car.

Wake up, folks! At a new car dealership or used car lot you are chum in shark-infested waters. The sales staff won't let you leave the lot until they have tapped every last dollar out of you that they possibly can. That means add-ons, options, extended warranties, paint sealer, carpet sealer and yes, the car loan financing.

You've decided on a new car and have filled out the purchase agreement. You now own the car but have to figure out how you will pay for it. That means a trip to the finance department. The finance person at a dealership will ask you a few personal questions and then type a lot of information into the computer between him and you. The finance person doesn't want to share this information. Smart consumers make smart decisions, but he wants to keep you stupid. Now a minute goes by and you start to get nervous, I know I do and I know I have good credit. But the finance person is still looking at your credit report on the computer screen. Credit reports by nature look pretty complicated; even if he let you look at the screen, you probably wouldn't know how to read it.

After a few moments the finance person knows all your financial secrets and history. Even if you have great credit, they will find a few bad things that he could point out to justify their next move. That is, adding on to the advertised low interest rate or advertised low monthly payment amount by either increasing the interest rate or adding service charges, banker's fee, application fees, credit fees and any other fees that he can convince you that you have to pay on top of the regular loan amount. The finance person may not even tell you that they have just loaded your loan up with all these added fees. The dealership is very good at burying these fees somewhere on the loan contract where you can't find them. The finance person is especially hard on people who do have bad credit. You know who you are, and now the finance person knows it too. They know you are vulnerable here. They can really gouge you on the interest rates and fees, all the time making it look like they're doing you a huge favor by giving you the money in the first place. The loan department is a profit center at car dealerships. That means that the loan department is required to present profits to the business.

CAR MANUFACTURERS MAKE ALMOST ALL OF THEIR <u>PROFITS</u> FROM FINANCING THE PURCHASE OF A CAR AND NOT FROM THE SALE OF A CAR.

The finance person may just offer you a payment amount and number of payments for the loan. You may feel so lucky to get a loan or you are so excited that you can now drive home the dream car you always wanted, you just say, "Yes!" to the loan proposal. Unfortunately, you probably just got ripped off.

So how can TVM help you out in this situation? You simply whip out the Texas Instruments BA II PLUS financial calculator you had in your pocket.

To start you turn the calculator on.

PRESS (ON/OFF)

Now you need to be sure that all of the information held in the TVM memory is cleared so it will contain no values. Press the (2nd) key, it's the lightest key on the calculator; you will be using the second function for each key so you **MUST** use the beige print just above the keys and printed on the calculator case.

PRESS (2nd)(QUIT)(2nd)(CLR TVM)

We need to specify how many payments per year we are dealing with. You may have just performed some calculations on bonds which make two interest payments per year. So to be sure we have it right, let's always do this repertory step. In this example we are going to be making 12 payments per year.

PRESS (2nd)(P/Y) it's the white I/Y key

There should be "P/Y=" on the left side of the display. If it is displaying "C/Y=" **PRESS the down arrow key,** next to (ON/OFF)

Now with P/Y on the left side, look over to the right side of the display. This is the number of payments per year. If this number is displaying 12, you're good to go. If it isn't, you will need to do the following steps.

PRESS 12 (SET) (QUIT)

You should have prepared your calculator before showing up at the car lot. Your BA II PLUS calculator is now ready to check the loan payment amount for the stated interest rate and added on fees. Now the finance guy may be starting to squirm. Ask him, "How many payments?" He will reply, "48," for a four-year loan, "60," for a five-year loan.

PRESS 48 (N) or 60 (N)

Ask, "What is the interest rate you will be charging me?" He will say, "5.0%."

PRESS 5.0 (I/Y)

NOTE: INTEREST RATES ARE JUST AS NEGOTIABLE AS THE PRICE OF THE CAR!

Ask, "What is the loan amount?" He will say, "$20,000."

PRESS 20000 (PV)

When you make the final payment on this loan, the loan will be paid or the loan balance will be zero.

PRESS 0 (FV)

Now my favorite part!

PRESS (CPT) (PMT)

PMT= -460.59 for a 48-month loan will appear on the display.

PMT= -337.42 for a 60-month loan will appear on the display.

Your payment for this loan should be $460.59 or $337.42. The number is negative because you have to take this amount out of your pocket each month to make the loan payment. If you are off by a few pennies, don't worry about it. Different ways of handling rounding of numbers are probably to blame. If the finance guy is offing you the payment of $460.59, you're good to go and do the deal. If not, nicely ask the finance person to recalculate their payment amount because it doesn't match what your calculator says it should be. If you can't get him to do that, ask the finance person to get the manager of the finance department.

Explain to the manager that you have a simple calculator, but it does extremely **precise time value of money calculations**. Both you and the finance person have the same loan information but have arrived at different payment numbers. Does he have a financial calculator to verify the computer calculations? Don't imply any wrong doing; you simply want to confirm your monthly payment amount and the information used to make the calculation on this loan.

You will win if you stay calm. Tell the finance person that you still want the car, but that you will have to arrange financing somewhere else. They will either remove the tacked on fees, lower their interest rate, or you should get the car loan elsewhere. If you have decent credit, ask the bank that you do business with to pre-approve you for a car loan and write down the terms of that loan. You have some bargaining power at the car dealership finance department. I once bought a car by merely writing a check for the down payment and telling the dealer I would have financing within one week. I drove the car off the lot and started shopping for a car loan. I took the best loan offer.

You just lowered your monthly payment, paid for the calculator, paid for this book and maybe paid for one of those pricey options added to your dream car! You will enjoy that car so much more KNOWING that you saved some money and didn't get ripped off in the financing.

One last note on this example. Have you ever considered walking into the financing department first and seeing what terms they will offer you on a loan before picking out the car? If they try to rip you off here, you know they will do the same with the car purchase. Just an idea.

Now that you know TVM has real-world applications. The time line is a great resource to visually show all cash flows and assumptions in a given situation. It is important to remember that a time line is specific to only one financial transaction and the cash flows MUST BE PREDICTABLE. Don't try to lump all your credit cards, car, and house payments on one time line; it won't work.

Author's note: As a reward for finishing this book I just purchased a new car from Parker Cadillac in Little Rock, Arkansas. I sat with Dave Parker and Mark Roberts with my manuscript in one hand and my trusty Texas Instruments BA II PLUS calculator in the other. I worked out the numbers to confirm my payment just as I have described it and the payment was off by two cents. The Dave and Mark were both staring at me the whole time. I finally let him in on what I was doing. I have to say that I was really treated with respect and dignity during the entire car buying process. Not enough to change my view on car salesman, but enough to know that I will continue to do business at this establishment.

Chapter 6

MAKING MONEY WITH BONDS

I probably don't have to tell you this, but bonds are just plain boring as an investment. Bonds are all about predictable cash flows, a set maturity date, basic math and contracts. Bonds have very little of the excitement and media coverage that equities have. The exception was the mortgage meltdown of 2007/2008. But bonds are a big part of a smart investment strategy. There are times when bonds' price appreciation will outperform equities, real estate, commodities, hedge funds, artwork, and collectable cars.

You just need to know the basics of bonds to start making smarter investment decisions:

- to create a portfolio of bonds to make capital gains

- to know when to buy bonds for income

- to create a portfolio of bonds to secure, predictable income stream

- to know when to buy bonds to offset a future predictable outflow of cash, like a down payment for a house or your child's college education.

BOND BASICS

Bonds are very different from stocks in many ways. Bonds are contractual in nature. Each bond issued is individualized to meet the issuing entity's needs. When you buy a **new issue**

bond, you are actually loaning money directly to the entity issuing the bonds. In exchange for the money, the entity borrowing those funds and issuing the bonds promises to:

- repay the PAR VALUE, usually $1,000, on the maturity date of the bond

- pay the holder of the bond contract (bondholder) predetermined interest payments on a set schedule

- agree to follow the covenants listed in the bond contract.

When you buy a bond after the original issue or in the secondary market, you are actually buying the bond contract from the current owner.

The maturity date is the date that the issuing entity will make the last interest payment on the bond issue and return to the bondholders 'PAR VALUE' or 'FACE VALUE'. Usually PAR VALUE is $1,000 per bond. If you hold ten bonds of a certain company, then the maturity value is $10,000. Most bonds when issued are for the length of twenty or thirty years to the maturity date. However, you can find new issue bonds ranging form 90 days, 180 days, 1 year, 2 years, 3 years, 5 years, 10 years, or 15 years.

Interest on a fixed-rate bond is a stated percent of par value and what days of the year it will be paid is specified in the covenants. Normally bonds pay interest twice a year, but you can find some that pay monthly or annually. The first interest payment is normally six months from the issuance date. The last interest payment is made at the same time as the PAR VALUE is returned to the bondholder.

If the bond is issued with a variable interest rate, then things get a little more complicated. The bond will be issued to track a specified interest rate index, like the LIBOR (London Inter-Bank

Offering Rate) or the FED Funds rate. The interest paid on the bond will be determined by the value of the selected interest rate index on a predetermined day of the year set by the contact. Added to the selected interest rate are a number of **basis points**. One basis point is equal to .01%, so 100 basis points is 1.00%. The better the credit rating of the issuing entity the lower the number of basis points added to the index value.

If you own a bond from a company which goes out of business, the bondholders will normally be higher than equity holders in the payout of assets sequence. This is because creditors get paid before the owners. The payout order if a company goes out of business is something like this. Every asset the company owns is sold, then employees wages get paid, taxes get paid, senior debt is paid off, collateralized debt is paid off, subordinated debt is paid off, preferred stock is bought back, and finally, if any money remains, it goes to the equity holders.

Quick Bond History

Back in the old days, when the most popular mode of transportation was a horse or train, you bought a bond that had these little square coupons printed on the bottom of the bond certificate. There were usually 60 of these coupons as most bonds were 30-year maturities. Every six months you had a coupon mature and your great-grandmother would clip the coupon right off the bond certificate and off to the bank she would go. The bank would then redeem the coupon and give her the interest payment. This was called a '**Bearer Bond**'. Interest and principal was paid to the bearer of the paper square interest coupon and the bond certificate upon maturity, no questions asked.

The bearer bond had several problems associated with it:

- If your grandmother forgot to take the paper interest coupon

116

to the bank ever six months, she wouldn't receive any extra interest on that coupon. So she could lose interest on her interest if she were going to reinvest that interest income.

- The person who brought in the interest coupon or bond certificate didn't have to prove ownership.

o What if the bonds were stolen?

o lost in a fire?

o just plan forgotten about?

No records were kept of the owners of these bonds and a lot of people lost their money when these bonds were lost, stolen or destroyed. Illegal syndicates loved to buy these bearer bonds up and cash them in. These syndicates would launder their illegal gains by purchasing these bonds. The proceeds from the bonds now have a legal traceable past. Today, you can't buy a bearer bond.

Bonds today are all electronic or '**Book Entry'.** Book entry means that someone somewhere keeps track of:

- every bond issued

- who the owners of the bond are

- where those bonds are held, usually at brokerage or in a bank account of some sort.

When an interest payment is made, it either goes directly into the account holding that bond or a check is sent to the owner's home address. The same thing happens when the bond matures; it's all automatically handled for you nowadays.

THE FOUR C's OF BONDS

Several other things to look at when buying bonds are the '**4 C's of bonds**': **Collateral, Covenants, Capacity and. Character.** Collateral and Covenants will be found in the bond contractual section. Capacity will be found in the company's financial statements. Character will be found in the board of directors and management of the entity issuing the bond.

Collateral is the issuing entity setting aside some of their hard assets, like a building or parcel of land, to back the repayment of the bond. These assets by contract can't be sold by the company unless the proceeds are used to retire this bond issue. In case of business failure, the sale of these collateralized assets would first be used to pay the bondholders claim against the company, and any money left over would go into the company's general pool of liquidation money to pay creditors.

Covenants are certain safeguards or contractual promises made by the issuing company. In case of some particular event occurring then the management of the company would agree to take a particular course of action. An example of this is if the building that was financed through this bond issue is destroyed. There may be a covenant in the bond contract that would spell out that management would have to:

- rebuild the building

- prepay or retire the bond issue from the insurance proceeds

- attach a new piece of collateral to the bond issue.

Another covenant is a '**sinking fund**' provision. This covenant would require the issuing entity to place a certain amount of money into specific escrow account called a 'sinking fund'. The sinking fund payment amount and time frame for making the payments would be listed on a detailed schedule.

When the time comes and the bond issue is ready to mature, there should be enough money in the sinking fund to pay off all bond certificates at par value.

Some tax-free municipal bonds may specify that the revenue from a specific project will be used to fund the interest payments; this would be called a '**revenue bond**'. An example may be a toll bridge or turnpike. The revenue collected in the tolls will be used to pay the upkeep, the interest on the loans and pay into a sinking fund to retire the bond issue. There may be a problem if revenue doesn't meet forecasts, and as the creditor you will normally end up on the short side.

One covenant that has really bitten investors in a low interest rate environment is a '**call provision**' in the contract. The call provision means that the entity issuing the bond has the right, after some set time period in the contract, to be able to 'call in' or prepay the principal back to the holders of the bond before the maturity date. Why would an entity want this in the bond contract? Well, if interest rates are high when the bonds are originally issued and ten years later interest rates are 400 basis points lower (4%), it would make sense for the entity that issued the bonds ten years ago to offer a new bond issue at a 400 basis point interest discount and then pay off the original bonds. This lowers the interest payments the entity has to pay by $4,000,000 a year for every $100,000,000 of debt outstanding, and that improves the bottom line.

Along with watching the maturity dates of the bonds you own, you need to watch the call dates. You don't want to be collecting a great interest rate only to have all of your bonds called in in a low interest rate environment. This provision only helps the issuing entity, so this means the interest rate on the bond with a call provision will also be slightly higher than a comparable bond without a call provision to compensate the investor for the risk of bearing the call provision. If a bond is called, there is usually a small premium over par value. The premium is normally 1% or 2% over the par value or $10 or $20 dollars.

Capacity is the issuing entity's ability to make the interest payments and repay the par value of the bonds they have outstanding. For this you will need to know a little accounting and how to read financial statements. I'm not going to get into this area for this book; maybe this would be another book at a later time. Just know that if the company has very little cash flow (revenue line on income statement), they had better have a lot of cash on hand to cover the interest payments and other bills that occur during the normal course of business. I usually use the Moody's or Standard & Poors published ratings to help determine Capacity.

Character refers to the issuing company's past performance of paying their interest, and their return of principal payments. It also takes into account how management will view making these payments in the future. If management has in the past missed interest payments or made poor judgments concerning their repayment of debt, then this will lower the company's credit rating, which in turn will increase the interest rate the company is required to pay for borrowing more money. For the non-institutional investor who lacks the ability to constantly monitor a non-investment grade corporate bond, you may want to concentrate your bond purchase to investment grade. Then choose a money manager/mutual fund to manage your junk bond/high-yield portion of your portfolio.

A general bond guideline is that if you have to assume some risk, you will be compensated with a higher interest rate. More risk in a bond would be longer time to maturity, no collateral, lower credit rating, no sinking fund, a call feature, a revenue provision, a highly leveraged balance sheet, decreasing revenues, a history of missing interest payments, and an ineffective management team.

BOND CREDIT RATINGS

There are several major bond-rating services. The most familiar to the average investor are either Moody's or Standard & Poors. They operate a little differently, but look at a large volume of information when issuing their ratings. Their credit rating system is not uniform. There are no set universal rules in bond or stock research that we as investors can look to for help. The entities financial information is viewed with each researcher's particular take on the results of a series of accounting and economic ratios.

Here is how Moody's and Standard & Poors agencies rate bond issuers.

	Moody	**Standard & Poors**
Investment Grade	Aaa	AAA
	Aa	AA
	A	A
	Baa	BBB
Junk/High Yield Bond	Ba	BB
	B	B
Default	C	D

A company, federal government, state government or local government usually has several bond issues out at one time. Each issue was probably used for a specific purpose. The more issues an entity has outstanding, the more money it owes. Some large companies have billions of dollars of debt outstanding. The more debt outstanding, the more interest payments they will have to make. Before investing in a company, you may want to check on the number of issues and the total debt it has outstanding. This information is found in the company's financial statements. This is also one of the factors the credit rating agencies use when determining how to rate a company's debt.

You can also use the debt rating to get a feel for the company you are considering equity investment in.

Don't use these rating systems as gospel either. There are quite a few examples of these agencies dropping the ball on staying current with company news and finances. Enron is a good example of a company going bankrupt with billions of dollars of hidden dept and still maintaining an investment-grade rating.

GOVERNMENT BONDS

There are all kinds of US Government bonds out on the bond market. US Government bonds are usually free from state and local taxes, but there is legislation being proposed that may change the tax status. If tax issues are part of your investment concerns, then you need to consult with a tax specialist before investing or making a particular investment. **The only government bonds that are backed by the full faith and credit of the United States Government are issued from the US Treasury and Ginnie Mae. ONLY THOSE TWO!** All other US government bonds have '**inferred backing**' but not specific backing of the federal government. These bonds include Fannie Mae, Freddy Mac, Farm Bureau, etc....

US Government bonds are some of the safest bond investments you can buy. The risk of default is almost zero. I tell clients that if their US Government bonds default, then there is no need for money. Our currency is no longer a viable means of payment for anything.

Government bonds also carry different names depending on maturity dates: Treasury Bills, Treasury Notes and Treasury Bonds. Government's Treasury Bills (T-Bills) are issued with a maturity of a few days to no more than 26 weeks. They are zero-coupon bonds. You buy at a discount to par value and at maturity you receive par value. More on zero-coupon bonds later. Treasury Notes are issued with a maturity from two, three, five years to ten years and pay interest semiannually. Treasury Bonds are issued with maturities over ten years and out as far as 30 years. These Treasury Bonds pay interest semiannually. The federal government had stopped issuing 30-year bonds for a time when interest rates were very high. They brought them back in a lower interest rate environment.

The most common Treasury investment used individually is the zero-coupon bond called 'saving bonds' or 'Series EE'. You can buy these at any bank or credit union. They sell for one half of par or maturity value. The maturity date is around twelve years. The maturity date is variable to the fluctuations of interest rates. The higher the current interest rate, the shorter time to maturity, and the lower the interest rate, the longer time to maturity. You will be told exactly when it matures when you buy a Series EE bond. You also have to hold them for at least six months before you can cash them in. The interest on these Series EE bonds is also taxable.

TIPS: TREASURY INFLATION PROTECTION SECURITY

Treasury Inflation Protected Securities, also known as TIPS, are securities whose principal is tied to the Consumer Price Index. With inflation, the principal increases. With deflation, it decreases. When the security matures, the US Treasury pays the original or adjusted principal, whichever is greater.

TIPS pay interest every six months based on a fixed rate

applied to the adjusted principal. Each interest payment is calculated by multiplying the adjusted principal by one-half the interest rate. Follow the links below to view detailed data on the CPI numbers for various time periods.

The following is a summary of the key provisions and features of these securities:

- The inflation-protected securities are structured similarly to the Real Return Bonds issued by the Government of Canada.

- The interest rate, which is set at auction, remains fixed throughout the term of the security.

- The principal amount of the security is adjusted for inflation, but the inflation-adjusted principal will not be paid until maturity.

- Semiannual interest payments are based on the inflation-adjusted principal at the time the interest is paid.

- The index for measuring the inflation rate is the non-seasonally adjusted US City Average All Items Consumer Price Index for All Urban Consumers (CPI-U), published monthly by the Bureau of Labor Statistics (BLS).

- The auction process uses a single-price auction method that is the same as that currently used for all of Treasury's marketable securities auctions. The securities are eligible for stripping into their principal and interest components in Treasury's Separate Trading of Registered Interest and Principal of Securities (STRIPS) program.

- At maturity, the securities will be redeemed at the greater of their inflation-adjusted principal or par amount at original issue.

- If, while an inflation-protected security is outstanding, the

CPI is (1) discontinued, (2) in the judgment of the Secretary, fundamentally altered in a manner materially adverse to the interests of an investor in the security, or (3) in the judgment of the Secretary, altered by legislation or Executive Order in a manner materially adverse to the interests of an investor in the security, Treasury, after consulting with the BLS, will substitute an appropriate alternative index.

All of the information in the TIPS section was taken directly from the US Department of The Treasury website.

MUNICIPAL GOVERNMENT BONDS

Municipal 'Muni' bonds are issued by state and local governments. These bonds are usually free from federal and state taxes as long as you live in the issuing state. The tax laws have changed quite a bit over the years. It's best to seek the advice of a tax planner to see if you can take advantage of the possible tax savings with these types of tax-free bonds.

Municipal bonds can also be insured using an independent insurance company, who will guarantee the payment of interest and principal. There are many such companies and I don't know if there is any real difference between them. These bond-insuring companies usually receive a portion of the bond issue for free in order to insure the entire bond issue. Keep in mind that the insurance is only as good as the company backing it. Insured municipal bonds are usually AAA rated. This insurance also reduces the coupon interest rate that the bond will pay because you are buying a pretty secure bond with little risk.

There is a very simple formula that you can use to decide if your **after-tax** rate of interest on a taxable bond is higher than that of a municipal bond:

(1 – your federal tax rate) X taxable bond rate

example:

You are looking at two bonds:

Bond 1: US Government 20-year paying 6.00%

Bond 2: Local county 20-year AAA rated and insured paying 3.50%

Your Federal tax rate is 33%

(1 - .33) X .06 =

(.67) X .06 = .0402 = 4.02%

NOTE: in math the % sign moves the decimal point over to the right 2 places so 6% = .06

The return you would get on a 6.00% taxable US government bond after accounting for taxes would be 4.02%. When comparing these two bonds after-tax returns the investor should choose the US Government bond at 4.02% vs. the Municipal bond at 3.50%. Both bonds have virtually no default risk, both are of the same maturity, and both pay semi-annual interest payments. This is a good example of comparing apples to apples once we make the adjustment for taxes.

CORPORATE BONDS

Corporate bonds are issued by businesses and other non-governmental organizations. Normally, corporations issue bonds to meet a specific need: to finance a new factory or some other very expensive project. But with the low interest rate of the early 2000's we have seen corporations issuing bonds just to take advantage of the low interest rate environment. These bonds have no set purpose, or very vague reasons for raising the money is listed. These borrowed funds will be held in very safe, secure investments until a project or acquisition is approved.

These funds can be used as leverage in making a deal happen. Would you as a seller of a business talk more seriously to the buyer who already has the money in the bank as opposed to one who has to start arranging for financing once terms are agreed?

JUNK BONDS a.k.a. HIGH-YIELD BONDS

Junk bonds are bonds issued by companies that are rated below investment quality. That means that the rating agencies perceive that there is some uncertainty about the issuing entity's ability to make the interest and principal payments. Now you won't hear these bonds being called junk bonds anymore. Wall Street has renamed them 'High-Yield Bonds', doesn't that sound a lot safer than 'junk bonds'. It may sound safer, but it sure isn't any safer for the investor. It is my recommendation that individual investors avoid this asset class. Why buy junk when you can buy a high-quality asset? If you decide to buy into this class, it would be safer to buy either a closed-end mutual fund or an open-end mutual fund. At least you will have a professional money manager and their staff keeping an eye on your investments.

FOREIGN BONDS

These are bonds issued buy foreign governments and corporations located outside of the United States borders. They may be issued in any world currency. There are many more major considerations to look at when considering a foreign bond: issuing entity risk, foreign exchange risk, country risk, political risk or possible trade barriers are just a few. If you decide to use a foreign bond as an investment, you should consult with an expert in this area. It is too easy to buy a bad bond. Needless to say that your portfolio should be well into the millions before entering this area, there are just so many good domestic bonds issued within this country to use.

Insurance companies are the biggest businesses in the world, and thus the biggest investors in bonds. I was lucky enough to interview for a job with a small New England insurance company in their bond department. I learned so much practical knowledge about investing and making money with bonds in the interviewing process. Insurance companies will buy bonds to meet their future predicted cash flows. They determine future cash flows by the type of insurance policies that they write and what the actuarial tables tell them about how much they expect to payout in claims. If the insurance company predicts they will have ten million dollars of claims due to be paid out in November 2015, then they will have ten million dollars of bonds maturing the month before to make the payout. Here the insurance companies match the predicted liability (claims) with a predictable maturing asset (bond). Of course insurance laws regulate how much of their assets can be invested in what asset class, and that is mainly using bonds.

Pension or retirement plans could use this same method of buying bonds to meet their monthly predicable pension payments, but pension plans are able to invest more of their money in equities. Equities are supposed to have a higher total return, so the company funding the pension doesn't have to deposit as much money into the pension. Pensions operate in a different legal environment than insurance companies. Pension plans are normally much more heavily weighted in equities. Pension plans also know what their payout liabilities will be in the future but choose to go after investment returns before the idea of offsetting liabilities.

If the company faced server fines or penalties for under-funding their pension, you would hear about fewer pensions failing and having to be taken over by the federal pension-guaranteeing agency. There is, however, some good news. As of August 2006 there is a bill waiting to be signed that makes businesses more liable for their under-funded pensions.

Another problem with most pension plans starts when the stock market has a few bad years and their pension plan assets suffer, like in 2000 to 2004. Pensions are a nightmare of bureaucracy which is meant to protect the people who rely on the pension. This bureaucracy makes it difficult to adjust the asset allocation of the pension, and doing so to reflect current market conditions requires meeting after meeting. Usually a watered down plan is approved, but it is not enough and too late. The people who rely on this plan to see them through their retirement years are the ones who suffer.

BOND TACTICS FOR THE LONG-TERM INVESTOR

Bonds have a predetermined maturity date, predetermined interest payment dates, predetermined interest rate and predetermined par value, which is usually $1,000. Where the heck can anyone make any money? You can't change the maturity date! You can't change interest payment dates! You can't change the interest rate! You can't change the par value! The only part of a bond that you **can** change is the buy/sell price on the secondary market. That is where you can make capital gains or losses on bonds.

The long-term investor doesn't need any income generated from their investments at this point in their life. How about investing in a bond that produces no interest income? Hmmmm, sounds kinda weird, a bond that doesn't make any interest payments. Well, there is such an animal and it's not for everyone, but it's called a 'ZERO-COUPON' or 'STRIPPED' bond. A regular interest-paying bond is 'stripped of the coupons' (a throw back to the days of bearer bonds where the coupons were clipped or stripped off the actual bond certificate) and then sold to someone who needs the income. Then the zero coupon bond is sold at a deep discount to par value and matures at par value, usually $1000.

A zero-coupon bond is a hybrid bond. It has a more thinly traded market than a coupon bond. This is not an illiquid market, but different rules apply to these bonds. The investor needs to be a little more knowledgeable and sophisticated. If you expect to sell a zero-coupon bond immediately, there will be a reduction in price. If you have a few days to let this bond sit on the market, the price should be 'bid up' a little. The same advice applies to a thinly traded equity. If an institution wants out of a thinly traded equity or bond, the price could plummet. If an institution wants to take a position in a thinly traded equity or bond, the price could skyrocket. The price of the investment will usually return to normal trading when the abnormal trading ends. Use these high trading volume times to your advantage. It's usually worth the wait.

The most common zero-coupon bond used by many today is the US Government Series EE saving bond. You pay 50% of the face value and are told when the bond will mature for the face value; it usually takes about 12 years for this bond to mature. The maturity date varies with the prevailing interest rates at the time of issue. Now let's see how you can make money on a 'Stripped' or 'Zero-Coupon' bond.

An example of a zero-coupon bond is in order. Let's say that ABC company is about to issue a bond for $1,000. It is set to mature in 30 years, pay 6% interest on the 15th of January and July. The price that you will pay for the new bond issue is $1,000. Current interest rates for companies of similar credit quality are also 6%. That's an important point because investors demand a higher interest rate for taking on more credit risk. Below is a timeline for this bond.

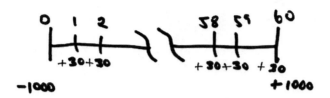

There are several large brokerage firms that buy new issue bonds and strip off the interest to be sold to one party, leaving the zero-coupon bonds for another party to buy. Now they don't do this out of the goodness of their hearts. This is Wall Street and greed is the order of business. No, these folks will add a little service fee here, raise the price to buy this specialty investment vehicle there, and in the end will make a few bucks on every bond. If you sell a few thousand of these a day, the money soon starts to add up.

OK, you bought the bond and paid $1,000 for it. But you really wanted a zero-coupon bond. So let's look at how we can price this bond as a zero-interest bond. First you have to separate the interest payments and the principal. The easy way is to buy a Texas Instrument BA II PLUS calculator and in a few entries you can get the same information.

N=60	number of payment periods
I/Y=6	interest rate bond pays
PMT=0	amount of interest income we receive
FV=1000	maturity value of bond
CPT PV=-169.73	price we are willing to pay in today's dollars for $1,000 in 30 years

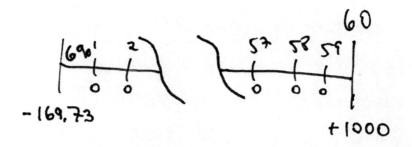

The answer is -$169.73, the number is negative because you have to pay out or incur a negative cash flow to buy the bond.

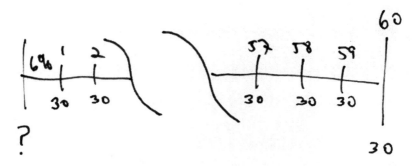

Now let's look at the other half of this bond, the income side. An investor who is retired and only concerned with interest and not really interested in tying up $1000 for 30 years would be interested in this type of investment. That investor will buy the income side of this bond. Here is the timeline of cash flows for this side of the bond.

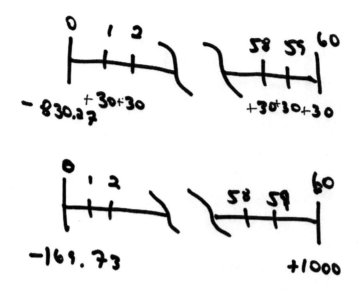

As you can see, the only thing missing from the timeline is the price that this investor will pay for the income stream. We will now figure that out with our trusty BA II PLUS.

N=60	interest rate bond pays
I/Y=6	interest rate bond pays
PMT=30	$1000 X .06 /2 amount of interest income we receive semiannually
FV=0	maturity value of income portion of the bond

CPT NPV= -$ 830.27 price we are willing to pay in today's dollars for 60 semiannual payments of $30

The income stream investor will pay $830.27 for 60 semi-annual payments of $30. The income stream totals out to $1,800 (60 X $30). To check our math and see if we are right, we will add the PV principal side of the bond with the PV interest side of the bond, and that should equal $1000.

PV Principal	$ 169.73
PV Interest Payments over next 30 years	$ 830.27
PV Total	$1,000.00

At the end of thirty years, your zero-coupon bond will mature for $1,000. But we all know that interest rates do not remain steady for very long.

What else does this example show us? You bought the zero-coupon bond at $169.73, which will mature in thirty years for $1,000. I know that it sounds unrealistic. You do nothing for thirty years you will have that much money. That's the power of the 30-year time-value component. If you are 35 years old and want to retire at 65 with $1,000,000 in the bank, in cash, it would cost you $169,730 today. Here's the math for this example:

$1,000,000 divided by $1000 par value bonds = 1000 bonds needed

1000 bonds needed times $169.73 PV of bonds= $169,730

No smoke or mirrors. Just a little bit of basic math and there it is. The problem is that most 35-year-olds don't have $169,730 in the bank to invest. What I have come to realize is that when presenting this investment scenario to a client it comes across as 'too good to be true'. The client is hesitant to commit to the idea of making that much money doing nothing, or committing the time required to realize maturity value.

Now that we understand the math and the power behind a zero-coupon bond, let's see another way how we as investors can make money with these hybrid bonds. So let's say that the very instant you bought your zero-coupon bond the interest rates jumped 2% up to 8%. This is a totally unrealistic circumstance, but it is to show how the price of your bond can change with interest rates. If we recomputed the price of the bond, it will show that if you had to sell this bond right now, you would get $95.06, a capital loss of $74.60 off the purchase price.

N=-60

I/Y= 8

PMT=0

FV=1000

CPT PV= $95.06

Let's look at it the other way. Say interest rates dropped 2% down to 4%. If we recomputed the price of the bond, we see that it is worth $304.78, a capital gain of $135.05

N=-60

I/Y= 4

PMT=0

FV=1000

CPT PV= $304.78

As you can see from the above example, you can make or lose money on bonds. An easy way to think about buying a bond for capital appreciations is to visualize a seesaw or teeter-totter with interest rates sitting on one side and the price of the bond sitting on the other.

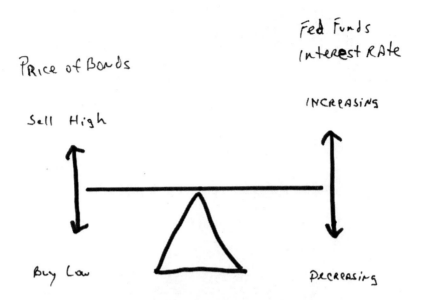

As interest rates rise, the price of the bond falls. This is because all you can change on a bond is the price you buy or sell it at; everything else is fixed by the contractual nature of the investment. You have to set the price of the bond lower so that the unchangeable dollar value of the current coupon being paid by the bond is equal to the current interest rate environment.

Think about it in another way. You have a 6% zero-coupon bond and interest rates rise to 8%. If you offered your bond for sale yielding 6% and someone was offering a zero-coupon bond that was yielding 8%, which bond would you buy? The 8% bond of course! But if you lowered the price on your bond so that the set coupon payment of 6% was now equal to 8%, the buyer would be indifferent as to which bond they would buy. He would receive an 8% return on both investments.

Now the long-term investor should be looking at 30-year bonds when interest rates are high to make capital gains. That's because the longer the maturity of the zero-coupon bond, the more volatile the price will be to changes in interest rates. If you looked at the price movement of a 30-year bond to a one-year bond, the same interest rate change would affect both bonds' price. The effect on the 30-year bond will be much greater. The long-term investor wants high capital gains so they choose the longest maturity possible to leverage volatility to their advantage.

Here's an example of that:

We will use our 30-year zero-coupon bond paying 6% semiannually; the current price is $169.73. Our one-year to maturity bond also pays 6% semiannually; its current price is $942.60. Interest rates go up 2% the 30-year zero-interest bond is worth $95.06 and the one-year bond is worth $924.56, (N=2, I/Y=8, PMT=0, FV=1,000, CPT, NPV=-924.56).

1-year	30-year
$942.60	$169.73
-$924.56	-$95.06
$18.04	$74.67

If interest rates dropped by 2%, then the 30-year bond would be worth $304.78 and the one-year bond worth $961.17 (N=2, P/Y=4, PMT=0, FV=1,000, CPT, NPV=-961.17).

1-year	30-year
$961.17	$304.78
-$942.60	-$169.73
$18.57	$135.05

Another factor that affects the price volatility of a bond is the stated coupon rate. The higher the stated coupon rate on the bond, the less volatility it will have on the price when interest rates change. Think of the high interest rate cushioning or acting as a buffer for price changes. The long-term investor wants high capital gains so they choose the smallest possible coupon rate possible to leverage this volatility to their advantage.

What happens when a zero-coupon bond is called?

If a bond issue can be 'called in' this will also affect the price. As interest rates decline, the company that issued debt instruments can refinance their debt at lower rates. They do this all the time and they 'call in' or prepay the higher interest paying bonds currently issued and reissue the debt at a lower interest rate. This will save money for the issuing company on its interest expense. As interest rates move lower, at some point in time investors know that these bonds can be called, and the bond price will be capped and maybe decline in value if interest rates go extremely low. Investors know the call price that will be paid by the issuing company will be the most these bonds are worth. The called amount will have to be reinvested at the current lower interest rate. The saving that the company makes in interest payments is your loss of interest income.

Now this looks a little different. The owner of a zero coupon bond would love to have that bond called. First, the zero-coupon bondholder won't have to wait the whole 30 years to get his $1,000. Secondly, the zero-coupon bondholder may get a premium of $10 or $20 dollars. Talk about a great deal! Now when someone gets a great deal on Wall Street, someone is also getting screwed and that would be the income stream holder. His income stream stops. *Puff!* It's gone. No more checks. That is a definite risk on the income side. Now if the income stream investor makes sure that they bought a non-callable bond, they are protected from this form of risk.

BONDS FOR THE TRANSITIONAL INVESTOR

If you have just become a transitional investor and interest rates start to decline, you can buy some zero-coupon bonds and get some capital appreciation out of them. But this should be the last time you use zero-coupon bonds until you have created a reliable income stream using high-coupon long-term bonds. You need to begin to think about creating a strong, safe and long-lasting, dependable income stream.

The transitional investor gets to play a waiting game. You will need to buy long-term bonds, maturity greater than 15 years, that pay a high dividend. Since you are planning ahead, you have time to wait for the right high interest rate environment to make a smart, unhurried and profitable investment purchase. These long-term high-interest-bearing bonds will need to be purchased when interest rates are high. How do you know when that is? The FOMC will tell you, if they are raising rates, you need to be patient. If they go from a raising interest environment to a lowering of interest rates, now is the time to buy! You should be able to lock in higher interest rates for less money. Also pay special attention to those call dates on your bond portfolio. Make sure the bonds you buy don't all become callable in the same time frame. If all your bonds are called in a low interest rate environment, you could be really stuck for years with low-paying bonds.

Here's a quick and easy chart you can draw out to visually see your maturity and call risk. I do mine on an easy excel spreadsheet chart. Each column represents one year and each row is the total value of bonds callable that year. I like to use the face value amount to show the size of the bond issue owned, and it also makes it easier to work the numbers on the spreadsheet. In this example I have 'laddered' the bonds to mature every year for five years. That's why the bond value decreases in the last five years of the chart.

BOND VALUE	YEAR MATURING	YEAR CALLABLE
$40,000	2025	2010
$40,000	2026	2001
$40,000	2027	2004
$40,000	2028	2008
$40,000	2029	2009

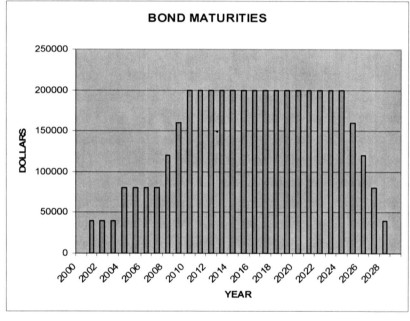

Laddering a bond portfolio spreads bond maturities over a specific time frame and at a specific time interval. This creates a portfolio that doesn't all mature in one year. Laddering can also increase interest income during a low interest rate environment. In this situation you could buy 6-month, 12-month, 18-month and 24-month maturity bonds. At the end of six months one of your bonds matures; you can now reinvest the proceeds into a 24-month, bond which should have a higher interest rate than a

6-month. Your portfolio is once again holding bonds that mature in six months, 12 months, 18 months and 24 months.

The same principle holds true to bonds in a high interest rate environment. Your time frames could be 22, 24, 26, 28 and 30 years until maturity. The only difference here is that you have to watch call features on the bonds and what months the bonds pay interest.

BONDS FOR THE INCOME AND GROWTH INVESTOR

Quality! Quality! Quality! Your speculation days are over except for a very small portion of your portfolio. Buy and hold good quality high-dividend-paying bonds. You can't survive a big hit in the value of your portfolio. Don't 'bet the farm' on any individual bond issue. If that company goes bankrupt, so could you. Be conservative, you have to be. Be smart, always!

Manage maturity dates and call features. If interest rates are high, there is no reason to have bonds in your portfolio of less than 25 years till maturity. You may never again in your life have this opportunity, take it. Watch over them like a farmer over their crops and reap the rewards of a great harvest over the years.

When interest rates are low or rising, buy bonds with shorter maturities. Buy bonds that you can hold to maturity so you won't lose principal (capital loses) if you have to sell early. When interest rates have risen, you can lengthen the duration or time to maturity of the bonds that you are now buying to take full advantage of locking in those higher interest rates again.

See, it really isn't all that hard. Follow the basics of bonds:

- High interest rates, buy long-term bonds
- Low interest rates, buy short-term bonds.
- Always watch call features

- Always buy quality.

LADDERING BOND STRATEGIES

Laddering bonds is an effective way to manage your maturities. Instead of buying one bond issue for your portfolio, you can spread out the maturities over several years. A common laddering technique would be to have equal amounts of one, three and five-year bonds. As the shortest maturity bond matures, you buy out five years again. The three-year bond is now a two-year to maturity bond and the five-year bond is now a four-year to maturity bond. In another two years the original three-year bond matures and you could buy another five-year bond. What this technique does is let you buy the longer-term bonds with usually higher-paying interest rates. In the end you should have a portfolio of five-year bonds set to mature in different years.

Chapter 7

EQUITY INVESTMENTS

With equities I like to start with the 'Big Picture'. I think about investing in equities much like menus at progressively more upscale dining establishments. The more money you have to invest, the more choices you can choose from. As your choices increase so does the sophistication needed to understand and monitor them.

Now I know many very wealthy families that don't think that they are as rich as they are. They want to keep their world simple and uncomplicated so they take a holistic approach to keep everything uncomplicated, which includes their investments. That is their wish and it works for them. Non-wealthy people on the other hand that have very little but act like they are wealthy is a recipe for disaster. I know in this world of 'Flash and Bling' it's tempting to live beyond your means. But from my dealings with wealthy people, they would love to go back to a simpler life. The paradox of wealth is that once you have it, everyone tries to take it away from you. I guess what I'm trying to say is, enjoy life right now and keep it simple.

Menu Page One

Investable Assets Under $5000

Come on in and have a seat. Basic meat and potatoes

Cash/Money Market

Savings Account

Checking Account

Nothing exciting here, these services fulfill the basic requirements. These three accounts will be built upon as your wealth increases. You will never outgrow these three accounts.

Menu Page Two

Investable Assets Over $5,000 but Under $250,000

Wait in line. Good predictable food. Nothing you can't figure out if you study the menu."

Cash/Money Market

Savings Account

Checking Account

Exchange Traded Funds (ETF).

Open-Ended Mutual Funds

Closed-End Mutual Funds

Individual Securities

These are still very liquid investments. Volatility in price is growing. Asset allocation needs to follow changes to interest rates.

Menu Page Three

Investable Assets Over $250,000 but Under $1,000,000

You will probably need a reservation. Fancy food, you will need a little help understanding the menu.

Cash/Money Market

Savings Account

Checking Account

Traded Funds (ETF)

Open-Ended Mutual Funds

Closed-End Mutual Funds

Individual Securities

Money Managed Accounts

<u>Advisors Needed</u>

Investment

Tax/accounting

Insurance

Legal

This is the time you will need to start assembling your personal life consulting team. I have nicknamed the personal life team the 'Dream Team'. You hire these people to help you achieve your dreams. They will be part of many of your biggest decisions for the rest of your life. Choose them carefully for their knowledge, connections and the experience they bring to help you with your personal decisions.

<u>Menu Page Four</u>

Investable Assets Over $1,000,000

You will need a reservation or know the maitre d to get seated. You will need to have the menu interpreted for you.

Tax/Accounting Advisor

Trust Advisor

Insurance Advisor

Legal Advisor

This is a big page to turn because it signifies a milestone. You have wealth! You better start thinking the way rich people think. Rich, successful people hire workers to do tasks for them. Rich successful people watch and manage. You will need to look at setting up a trust and how you want to transfer your wealth to your heirs. Many very specialized investment vehicles will be available to you. You just don't have the time to educate yourself on all the available investment, following the investments and tracking the investments so hire someone to do it for you.

INDIVIDUAL EQUITY ASSET CLASSES

This book will discuss the generalities of the main equity asset classes. I use the word 'generalities' because within every class there are exceptions, and I won't be discussing those. I want to leave you with the 'Big Picture Concepts' on what to expect if you owned a basket of more than 15 or 20 individual stocks in each of the asset classes below:

Market Capitalization is one method to categorize individual equities. It's the value you get when you multiply the number of shares outstanding or tradable for a company times the current market price. Generally speaking, a large-cap company is over 10 billion dollars. A mid-cap company is between 2 and 10 billion dollars. A small-cap company is between 300 million and 2 billion.

The major asset classes I will focus on are:

LARGE-CAP VALUE

LARGE-CAP GROWTH

MID-CAP

SMALL-CAP

INTERNATIONAL

Generally speaking, the most price-volatile stocks are at the bottom of the list above. They get less volatile in price as you go up the list. Large-Cap Value stocks are large mega-sized companies. They should be in a mature stage where you expect income in the form of a dividend and some price appreciation. Slow steady price movement is what you are looking for.

Large-Cap Growth stocks are also a mega-sized company. The difference is that these companies pay little or no dividend. They are reinvesting the money they could be paying out as dividends back into the company. Reinvestment should equate into a higher value of the company and thus a higher price of the stock in this company. Expect more price volatility than the large-cap value stocks.

A Mid-Cap company is hopefully growing, and growing pretty quickly. They have a new product, service, or process that does something better or faster. They are well past the start-up phase but still have a lot of market share available to grow into. They have a recognized product or products. The question is not if they will survive, but how smart they will grow or if they will be bought by a mega-sized company. The difference between a value and growth mid-cap is an arbitrary set of financial ratios and their interpretation. Some more common financial ratios are price of stock/share earnings (P/E), price of stock/book value of stock (price to book) or price of stock/sales (price to sales).

Small-Cap companies can be considered start-ups. They have a product or service, but it is not either widely known or accepted. The company needs to get the word out on how much better their product or service does its job. At the same time the company needs to make sure that it will have enough products available. This is a very fine balancing act with limited financial resources. The difference between a value and growth small-cap is the same financial ratios used for mid-cap equities.

International equities are any company headquartered outside of your country. They can and are large, mid and small in size. With international companies come the added risk in the currency exchange rate of the home country, political stability and risk, economic risk of the country and region, trade barriers or restrictions that may be imposed. You could own the best investment in the world only to have their government realize the same thing and nationalize it. *Puff!* Your money is gone. Luckily, that is the exception.

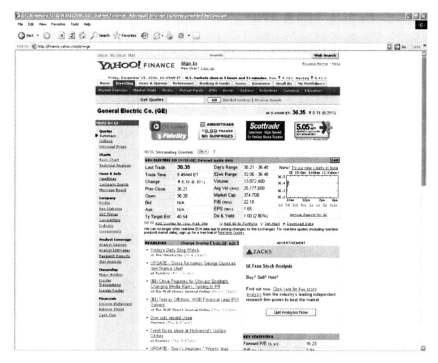

Above is the Yahoo financial page on General Electric. Everything that you see is free! This is my personal favorite finance site. There is so much information gathered here that I rarely need to look elsewhere. I'm a registered user and I keep all of the stocks I track and follow on my personal quote page. I can access this anywhere in the world, any time, and from any computer. I like that kind of unlimited access. The articles and commentaries are a bit weak, but there are many other places that I peruse for that content.

Bloomberg

Yahoo news

Market watch

MSNBC

INVESTING IN INDIVIDUAL EQUITIES

Investing in equities can take several forms. You can buy individual securities yourself, get a managed account where an outside manager buys in your account, or go with a pooled investment like a mutual fund.

DO-IT-YOURSELFERS

Do-it-yourselfers have seen many new online companies catering to their specific needs. You know what you want and how you want it. This book doesn't address many of your needs except in the chapter on placing an intelligent trade. For the do-it-yourselfers, remember that asset allocation is the main driver of returns, not stock selection. Market timing only creates a new way to lose your money. I can speak from experience having lost my own money trying to time the market.

Find someone you can honestly talk to about your investments. It may make perfect sense in your mind, but the logic falls apart when trying to explain a new trading idea to someone else.

Be prepared to spend way too much time tracking and researching investments. If you like to do this, great, go for it. If you don't, that's a good sign not to go there! Investing your money will also take on an emotional slant. The hardest account I manage is my parents' account. That's because I have an emotional attachment to my parents and want to make every trade a profitable one. Just for the record, that's impossible. Having someone else manage your assets takes some of the emotional strain out of investing.

INDIVIDUALLY MANAGED ACCOUNTS

Institutions and wealthy individuals don't put their money into mutual funds because they have the financial power to get the same services for a lot less in fees than the mutual fund buyer pays. The institutions and wealthy individuals get many more services, perks and lower taxes than mutual fund investors. Individually managed accounts have minimum account sizes. For equity it can be as low as $100,000, but for fixed income it is usually over $1,000,000.

You have to open up an account and deposit money into it. The money manager usually has the say as to what institution is the custodian of the account. The manager is given access to trade in your account by a contract both you and the manager sign. Usually either party can cancel the contract. The manager can also deduct their fees for managing the account, usually quarterly and at a fee schedule detailed in another contract. You have little or no say as to what is bought and sold in the account. The manager has full discretion on all transactions. Full discretion means that they can trade an account as often as they want without contacting you for approval.

An individually managed account pays fees on assets under management. If the value of your investments goes down, the manager makes less money. If the value of your investments goes up, the manager makes more money. I have never met a money manager who didn't want to make more money, therefore they have a vested interest in seeing your portfolio grow.

Most money managers have a specific kind of investing that they do. For me, I'm an asset allocator. I determine a client's risk tolerance and use that information to apply an asset allocation model. I pick the investments in that model using a specific set of guidelines. I rebalance portfolios on a set schedule, usually quarterly.

Some other money managers only invest in fixed income. They have found that they can beat the bond market with their trading guidelines and focus all of their effort in that area. Other money managers may invest in equities only. It could be in any group of equities or a niche area like small-cap value stocks. I have used these specialized money managers in the past with very good results as long as I only invested in their niche area.

POOLED INVESTMENTS

Pooled investments are investment vehicles where many people put their money into one investment basket. A fund manager invests the funds in the basket into individual investments. The fund manager is guided by the funds' stated investment objective. Pooled investments include: closed-end mutual funds, open-end mutual funds and Exchange Traded Funds (ETF). This type of investing gives the normal everyday people the investing power of huge institutions. Investors get instant diversification by holding a portfolio of many different companies. They get professional money management from the fund manager controlling the buying and selling positions in the portfolio. You also get all the research and brainpower from the investment firm once you own one of their funds in the family. You can find a pooled investment that covers any investment style, international region, or mirroring any index.

There are many places that can tell you about the size of an equity or equity mutual fund (ETF).

http://www.morningstar.com/

Morningstar is a membership-required site with tons of free information. If you know the symbol of a mutual fund, it will give you a page of many important decision-making pieces of information.

Fund Manager of the Year
Domestic Equity

Performance more ▶▶

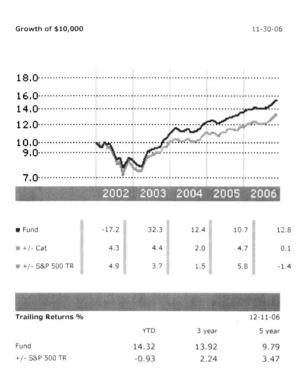

Growth of $10,000   11-30-06

	2002	2003	2004	2005	2006
■ Fund	-17.2	32.3	12.4	10.7	12.8
▩ +/- Cat	4.3	4.4	2.0	4.7	0.1
▩ +/- S&P 500 TR	4.9	3.7	1.5	5.8	-1.4

Trailing Returns %   12-11-06

	YTD	3 year	5 year
Fund	14.32	13.92	9.79
+/- S&P 500 TR	-0.93	2.24	3.47

The first is a chart with the price movement of a $10,000 investment. Added are the S&P 500 and a representative aggregate category index so you can do some very easy comparison to tracking two indexes and get a feel for the volatility in price. At the bottom of the graph are yearly return numbers followed by year to date (YTD), three-year and five-year average performance if the fund has been around long enough.

To the right of the chart is the key stats information.

Key Stats more ▶▶

Morningstar Category   Morningstar Rating

Large Blend	★★★★
NAV (12-11-06)	**Day Change**
$38.25	$0.08
Total Assets($mil)	**Expense Ratio %** ▶▶
42,374	0.87
Front Load %	**Deferred Load %**
4.75	None
Yield % (TTM)	**Min Investment**
0.71	$1,000
Manager	**Start Date**
Christopher Cullom Davis	10-01-95
Kenneth Charles Feinberg	05-01-98

This is a very important set of information. This tells you exactly what size company category this mutual fund invests in: large-cap, mid-cap and small-cap. This also tells you what investment style this mutual fund invests in: value, blend (a mix of value and growth) and growth.

Morningstar rates on a five-star system. One is poor and five is excellent performance. All rating services use different standards to rate investments. I use the philosophy that I do not want to invest my money in a one, two or three Morningstar 'star-rated' mutual funds. I will look seriously at a four of five-star rated funds. That doesn't mean that all one, two or three-star rated funds are bad. It just means that I won't invest my or my clients' money there.

Other important information to know is the expense ratio. This is the total charges that the mutual takes from you to manage and trade the fund. The lower the better, more money stays in your pocket. These fees are automatically deducted from your account either monthly or quarterly. You will never see them taken out, it just happens and you need to know that it does happen.

Front load is the amount of the investment that is taken from the money you invest in the fund. This amount typically finds its way into your financial planner/stockbroker's pocket. This is typical for an 'A' class of share. If you invest more than $25,000 in the A class shares, you may be entitled to a reduced front-end load. It's called a 'breakpoint'. It can save you a good chuck of money. There are few reasons to buy the A class shares. The two main points are a reduced expense ratio and your broker gets a big commission. My problem with big upfront commissions is that the broker already has his money. There is absolutely no incentive for this person to work for you. They will not receive another cent in commissions on this money until a few years down the road when they try to get you to move the money to another fund family so they get another big commission.

Deferred load is the amount your account will be charged if you take your money out before a set period of time. This is typical for a "B" class of share of a mutual fund. Usually the maximum amount of the deferred load is the commission your financial planner/stockbroker gets. Another big upfront commission for the broker, with no incentive to watch your investment.

Yield is the amount of money in percent that the investments inside the mutual fund pay out in dividends. This had more importance a few years back when it was taxed less than capital gains. It still is important for investors looking to invest for moderate growth and lots of income. $10,000 times .71% or .0071 = $71. This investment doesn't pay much in dividends. The main source of increase in your investment will be in price appreciation, not dividend income.

At the bottom are the mutual fund managers and their start date as fund managers. I will not use any performance number before the current manager started. Those performance numbers reflect the previous manager's performance. A new portfolio manager will piggyback the current investments for a few months after taking over a fund. By then the new portfolio manager will have adjusted the mutual funds holding to reflect their style of investing. If I am invested in a mutual fund that undergoes a portfolio manager change, I will be very active in looking to move all of my clients' money out of the mutual fund. Capital gains taxes in that case will dictate how aggressively I move.

The exception is when the mutual fund uses a very strict quantitative model that ranks or filters the investment universe of the fund. Quantitative models can be very simple but are normally extremely complex formulas that look at mountains of individual company information: how that companies reacts to certain economic environments, how that company moves with the current portfolio, where the manager thinks the economy will go, which direction will interest rates go, how this company reacts to interest rates changes, what category the company is in, what the forecast for that category is, etc... The amount of questions and the weighting that are given to them are infinite.

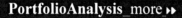

Morningstar Style Box ⑦

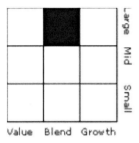

Average Mkt
Cap $Mil
37,874

Price/Prospective
Earnings
13.7

Ownership Zone ⑦

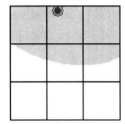

Fund centroid
represents weighted
average of domestic
stock holdings

Zone represents 75% of
fund's domestic stock
holdings

Above is a standard nine-cell block that describes the capitalization going vertical. Larger capitalization companies at the top and smaller capitalization companies at the bottom. On the horizontal axis is the investment style. Value indicated on the right side, Growth on the left side and a blend of the two in the middle. You should notice in the ownership zone block that this fund does invest in some mid-cap companies leaning towards growth

Asset Allocation % more ▸▸

Cash	1.6
Stocks	98.2
Bonds	0.3
Other	0.0

Above is the asset allocation of this fund. A sum of 98.2% in equities indicates that this is a pure equity fund, no fixed income. The manager is holding very little cash, which tells me they believe that the market is strong and don't want to hold too much cash. A mutual fund has to hold some cash to be able to handle the inflows and outflows of daily transactions when investors deposit and withdraw money. Cash is a drain on performance when the stock market is hot. The portfolio manager wants to hold little to no cash in up markets and maximum cash in down markets.

Sector Breakdown (% of stocks)

☞	**Information**	**10.88**
⬆	Software	2.04
▣	Hardware	1.42
●	Media	5.67
▤	Telecommunications	1.75
☞	**Service**	**57.64**
●	Healthcare	3.24
▤	Consumer Services	8.16

🗈	Business Services	5.07
💲	Financial Services	41.17
🖴	**Manufacturing**	**31.48**
🚗	Consumer Goods	13.09
⚙	Industrial Materials	6.21
🔥	Energy	12.18
💡	Utilities	0.00

Annual Turnover %   6

% Assets in Top 10   38.28

Annual turnover is an important tax number. In this fund, 6% of the fund assets are sold and the money used to buy other investments. This is very low and very tax efficient. Tax efficient means you will pay low taxes each year on this fund. Yes, any transactions generating capital gains, which are taxable in the year they are realized, are passed through the fund to the investors in the fund. It is typical to see turnover rates of 200% to 300% in small-cap funds or bond funds. If taxes are an issue with you, then this is a piece of information that you need to know.

Assets in the top ten refer to the weightings of the top ten holdings. The more weight or larger percentage, the bigger the bets made on the best picks. In this case 38%, over 1/3, of the fund rests on the performance of ten companies. A good or bad pick here can have big performance ramifications. There isn't a listing that gives the total number of investments, but the asset allocation portion can be expanded to reveal the top 25 positions and their weighting.

EXCHANGE TRADED FUNDS

An easy way to think of ETFs is that they are a mutual fund that trades like a stock, on an exchange. You pay a commission to buy them and sell them. If you bought shares in the ETF holding the Dow Jones Industrial Average (DIA - pronounced Diamonds), you own a small part of all 30 stocks in that one share. ETFs are usually non-managed portfolio of individual equities that mirror an index or specific sector.

You can buy the Standard & Poors 500 indexed mutual funds or all 500 stocks in SPY (pronounced Spiders) that trades on the American Stock Exchange (AMEX) and is the largest EFT. SPY has internal fees of .18%, that is very low for a pooled investment due to no active management of the holdings. Turnover, the percentage of the portfolio that is sold annually, around 6%, is very tax efficient. This ETF trades in very high volumes, it is very liquid. It holds 500 stocks, it is diversified. ETFs trade all day long, not just at the end of the day like mutual funds. You can use limit orders on ETFs. Since they trade like a stock you will be charged a commission to buy and sell the shares.

Here is my list of my favorite ETFs:

NAME	**SYMBOL**	**EXCHAGE**
Standard & Poors 500 Index Depository Receipts	SPY	AMEX
Diamonds Trust:	DIA	AMEX
NASDAQ-100 Trust Shares	QQQQ	NASDAQ
iShares Dow Jones Select Dividend Index	DVY	NYSE

Standard & Poors 500 Index Depository Receipts (SPY)

This ETF contains the 500 stocks in the S & P 500. It is the biggest ETF, trading roughly 80 million shares a day. It pays around a 1.7% yield and has annual expenses of .18%.

Diamonds Trust (DIA)

This ETF hold the 30 stocks in the Dow Jones Industrial Average. These are all very large, well-known blue chip companies. This pays a dividend of around 2% and has annual expenses of .18%.

NASDAQ-100 Trust Shares (QQQQ)

This ETF holds 100 of the largest NASDAQ traded stocks and it also trades on the NASDAQ. These pay almost no dividend and have annual expenses of .20%.

iShares Dow Jones Select Dividend Index (DVY)

This ETF holds the top 100 dividend-paying stocks in the Dow Jones Total Market index, excluding Real Estate Investment Trust (REITS). This pays over 3% dividend and has annual expenses of .40%.

It is off of these four ETFs that I like to build the foundation of an equity portion of a portfolio. I still use some mutual funds for international holdings and some individual stocks. But I believe it is very important to build a strong core group of holdings concentrated on diversity and quality before you can venture off into individual stocks.

OPEN-END MUTUAL FUNDS

Open-end mutual funds are a pooled investment that trade once a day, after the markets have closed. They calculate the Net Asset Value (NAV), the total worth of the portfolio after the market closes, and then divide that number by the number of shares outstanding. That gives the price per share of an open-end mutual fund. Once the share price is established, all buy and sell orders are executed at that price. After all buy and sell orders have been filled, trading stops until the next close of the markets when the same process will occur again.

There is no limit to the number of shares an open-end mutual fund can issue in the fund for sale. That is why some open-end funds close to new investors. The funds have grown so large that they have difficulty investing the money they have. The fund manager simply decides to close these funds to new investors.

There are many different classes to open-end mutual funds. There are load and no-load companies. Load mutual funds pay a broker or intermediary to sell their funds. These are usually in A, B, and C classes. A class shares charge the client 5% upfront. If the client buys $1,000 of A class shares, then the fund company takes $950 and buys the fund, then gives the $50 to the broker who sold the fund. The A class shares usually don't have any other broker compensation. If you have more than $100,000 to invest, you will need to look at the mutual fund company's policy on breakpoints. It could save you thousands of dollars.

B class shares are back-end loaded. If the client buys a B class share, all of their money goes into the fund. The company pays the broker who sold the fund $50. The back-end fee occurs if you take your money out of that fund family before a certain time frame, usually five or six years. You will be charged up to 5% of the deposit value on redemption. After the back-end time frame is up, the shares should convert to A class of shares, which usually have a lower internal fee structure.

C class shares have only a one-year back-end load and it's usually 1%. These shares pay the broker 1% a year. I like this share class. While you do in the long run pay a little more in fees, you pay as you go. I've seen people with A or B class shares convinced to sell their shares and endure a sales charge only to be placed in another similar class share somewhere else. These trades only made money for the people selling them.

No-load fund companies don't pay outside brokers or agents to sell their funds. You will usually save about 1% a year in fees. There are some no-load funds with higher internal fees than a load fund. When looking at fees you need to compare apples with apples. International funds should have the highest internal fees. This is due to the size of the staff that is needed to run one of these funds. Equity funds are next expensive with bond funds the least expensive internal fees. Internal fees pay for personnel, trading costs, marketing, and yes, profits to the fund company.

Open-end mutual funds trade with a five-letter symbol that always ends in an 'X'. Each mutual fund also has a CUSIP number for each class of share. When you get a quote on an open-end mutual fund, it will always be the closing price of the last trading day. If it's noon on Tuesday, you'll get the Monday closing price until the markets close on Tuesday.

Mutual fund managers actively manage the investments in their funds, and they have guidelines they have to follow which are spelled out in the fund prospectus. That is a very hard document to read. There is a movement towards 'plain English' when drafting these documents. I hope it happens soon.

Mutual fund managers get paid in many ways, but the main ones are assets under management. Assets under management are the total dollar value of the mutual fund. The more money that the mutual fund controls, the more money the manager makes. So a hot-performing mutual fund will see a lot more inflows of investment dollars, growing the assets under management. This means the manager gets more money for doing the same job. If the mutual fund has a bad quarter, then outflows of investment dollars would occur as those dollars seek a better returning investment, therefore lowering the managers earning. So the manager of a mutual fund has an interest in the assets under management.

Mutual fund managers' performance bonuses are usually measured on a quarterly basis. If they beat the index, like the S&P 500 or Russell 2000, then they get a bonus. The bonus could grow the more they beat the index. What this means for the mutual fund investor is that your large capitalization mutual fund could actually be a mid-cap biotech fund because that's the hot sector this quarter. You get the returns, the manager gets the money, but in the end you don't own a large-cap fund. Now some fund families are looking to make the fund manager more accountable for the make-up of the fund holdings.

It's called 'fund drift', or the gradual movement away from the basic investment style of your mutual fund or management style for individually managed accounts towards an area that is producing higher returns. Hey, the managers of your money aren't the only ones to blame. If you weren't so concerned about short-term returns as a consumer, moving your investment dollars from a not slumping fund to today's HOT fund, this problem wouldn't be so bad. If you as a consumer demanded that the manager manages your money by the guidelines outlined in the prospectus, you would actually get a growth fund and not a tech fund, which is what most funds were in the late 1990's before the stock market bubble burst.

Some mutual fund families have actually started measuring fund drift and using a financial incentive to ensure that the manager is following the investment guidelines of the prospectus. The fund manager has their pay or bonus adjusted downward the further away from the investment guidelines his fund holdings stray. How do you know what the biggest holdings are in the mutual fund? Look on the website. Don't expect up-to-date information, mainly because investors have demanded it. Holdings of a mutual fund are usually updated quarterly.

Window dressing occurs just before the end of the quarter. The fund manager will sell off some of the most out-of-guideline investments and buy investments within the mutual fund guidelines just before the end of the quarter. This makes the quarterly updates look as though the manager is managing by the guidelines, but in fact that may not be the case. This has become a little less of an issue as more information is disclosed about the portfolio holdings from the mutual fund companies.

Mutual fund managers may also be managing more than one mutual fund. The manager of the mutual fund may also manage separate individual accounts for wealthy individuals and institutions like pension funds for the same mutual fund company or with the fund manager's own investment company. Mutual fund companies like to stay with a winner. If they can put a star investment manager's name on another mutual fund, they will do it. They will brand this manager's name with theirs. But they will be careful here. A manager's hot streak can end quickly and the mutual fund company has no choice but to fire that now-losing manager and hire today's hot manager. It's nothing person, it's just how Wall Street works. Fund managers normally don't have much allegiance to a mutual fund. If a better offer comes along, they will normally take it. Remember Wall Street is built on GREED!

The institutions and wealthy individuals don't put their money into mutual funds because they have the financial power to get the same services for a lot less in fees than the mutual fund buyer pays. The institutions and wealthy individuals get many more services, perks, and lower taxes than mutual fund investors.

Another important issue to bring up is investing internationally. Our world is getting smaller and there are opportunities everywhere to make money. As an investor you need to think about investing internationally. This is one area where I like to use mutual funds as my investment of choice. International mutual funds from the largest mutual fund companies have invested huge amounts of resources here. I believe that an international fund by the very physically and cultural distances needs to be managed by team members who follow a certain geographical area.

CLOSED-END MUTUAL FUNDS

The shares of a closed-end mutual fund trade on a stock exchange like an ETF. You will pay a commission on every buy and sell transaction. A closed-end fund can only issue a set number of shares on its initial public offering (IPO). The shares of closed-end funds normally trade below NAV or 'at a discount'. Some hot closed-end funds could trade at a premium, above NAV, but that is rare. Portfolios of closed-end funds are usually actively managed by the fund manager. Blackrock and Vanguard are two large closed-end fund companies.

NON-POOLED INVESTMENTS

PREFERRED STOCKS

A preferred stock is a hybrid stock and bond. It is issued as a stock and trades on an exchange. It has a trading symbol and CUSIP. It is also supposed to last forever, like an equity. If you find a new preferred stock issue, you can buy them without paying a commission. Otherwise they trade like a stock with a commission for each time you trade them.

Preferred stock has a stated interest; it pays and set dates that it will make the interest payments. This is very much a bond characteristic. Remember, the dividends that an equity pays have to be approved by the board of directors each time they are paid. There is no certainty to an equity dividend. Most preferred stocks make their interest payments quarterly, but some can be found that pay monthly.

Preferred stocks are also priced like a bond. The price of a preferred stock rises in a lowering interest rate environment, and in a rising interest rate environment the price declines. The quality of the company issuing the preferred stock also contributes to price volatility, again like a bond. A company with a good credit rating will pay less stated interest and will be less price-volatile. Quality does count here.

EQUITY INVESTING FOR THE LONG TERM INVESTOR

ASSET CLASS	CONSERVATIVE	AGGRESSIVE
LARGE-CAP VALUE	30%	10%
LARGE-CAP GROWTH	30%	10%
MID-CAP	10%	20%
SMALL-CAP	10%	20%
INTERNATIONAL	20%	40%

The long-term investor is primarily looking for growth in the value of their portfolio. The long-term investor has a long time horizon, greater than ten years, so they can and should accept a little more price volatility (risk). I would start with your core investments with QQQQ and the SPY.

In a lowering interest rate environment, I would add the DIA and DVY. These large companies tend not to be beaten up as much as the tech stocks. Dividends will support the portfolio value a little. The long-term investor should have up to 40% in international, and some of that can be in emerging markets.

EQUITY INVESTING FOR THE TRANSITIONAL INVESTOR

ASSET CLASS	CONSERVATIVE	AGGRESSIVE
LARGE-CAP VALUE	35%	25%
LARGE-CAP GROWTH	35%	25%
MID-CAP	5%	10%
SMALL-CAP	5%	10%
INTERNATIONAL	20%	30%

The Transitional investor will want to be increasing their percentage of dividend paying DVY allocation and larger capitalization DIA and SPY allocation over the next ten years. Be smart and use market cycles to move and reposition your money. The transitional investor should continue to hold international but start reducing the percentage allocation and eliminate emerging markets all together.

EQUITY INVESTING FOR THE INCOME AND GROWTH INVESTOR

ASSET CLASS	CONSERVATIVE	AGGRESSIVE
LARGE-CAP VALUE	60%	40%
LARGE-CAP GROWTH	20%	20%

MID-CAP	5%	10%
SMALL-CAP	5%	10%
INTERNATIONAL	10%	20%

The income and growth investor will definitely want to look at holding some DVY and DIA. The dividends and large capitalization of the companies should make the portfolio less price volatile. As the direction in interest rates changes you should hold these and make adjustments with the balance of the equities. The Income and Growth investor should have no more than 20% in international equities and be totally out of emerging markets.

Chapter 8

INVESTING IN YOUR RETIREMENT PLAN

OK, so you now you have a good working knowledge of investing and asset allocation. That and $3.00 will get you a cup of coffee at Starbucks.

Most people never really comprehend the idea that the dollar amounts they see on their retirement statements are real or that this money belongs to them. This has led to some very poor decisions regarding their saving for retirement and retirement investing. You may participate in the 401k plan where you work, but the money you put into that plan and any IRA (Individual Retirement Accounts) accounts you have are **Your Retirement Plan**. The Money is real! The Plan is real! Your Retirement is real! You have to get this idea and concept into your head that **your retirement plan** is very real and it is very important. This isn't play money in **your retirement plan**! **Your retirement plan** may be a pain in the ass, but it's your ass on the line here!

You'd better believe that when you get close to retirement age, **your retirement plan** is going to get very, very, very real! It will happen very fast and hit you like a ton of bricks. You'll be somewhere, usually grocery shopping, and suddenly notice it. All the bag boys are old men. Men who didn't save enough for retirement and now they have to work for the rest of their lives to survive. They don't get to enjoy their retirement, survival is the best they can ask for until they can't work anymore and then it is charity time until they die.

You'll need to take a real worldview of **your retirement plan**. You will be spending lots of brain computing time on this subject over your lifetime. Trust me in this; investing in your retirement plan will get easier over time. That's because you will get better at investing over the years to come. Like any skill you learn along life's path, at first the task looks too hard to accomplish, but soon after you have mastered the basics the task is very manageable. Don't let others who will be bagging your groceries later in life drag you down into their misery.

I've first introduced you to and then ranted about the importance of **your retirement plan**. It's time to dispel some 401k myths, mainly excuses, I've encountered that others have used to justify not participating in the 401k plan where they work.

The first myth I hear is: "I put my hard-earned money into the 401k plan and as soon as my money hits the account it now belongs to the company."

Wrong! The money does come out of your paycheck, you earned it, and this money is always yours. There is a short period of time that the company holds your money for you before depositing it into your retirement account. This is strictly an administrative function to save on some of the costs of the plan. The money is always earmarked for you. The money is always accounted for by the bean counters, who by the way put their own money into the plan as well.

There are several accounting techniques for handling the money inside a 401k. One method is the pooled method. It's like investing in a mutual fund. All the money is first accounted for by each person in the retirement plan and is then thrown into one big bucket. That money is invested according to your wishes. I know it sounds weird, but it is again very cost effective, which means you pay less in fees. Like your bank account and mutual funds, every penny in there is accounted for so don't worry about your money disappearing.

Another way to account a 401k is to have actual separate accounts. Your money is segregated from all others but is pooled together at the investment level in mutual funds. In the end most 401k's invest in mutual funds so your money will be pooled with that of others. We have the best laws in the world to protect your money in these investments, and they work.

You may be reading this and say, "Wait, I put my money into my retirement plan and I can't get it out if I need it." That's right; this money is in a 'retirement account' or a bank account or checking account. Bank or checking accounts are demand accounts. You can go to any bank branch and demand your money whenever the banks are open. Retirement accounts are closed to withdrawals until you 'retire'. This is to prevent them from becoming demand accounts. Yes, I know that there are certain circumstances that you can take money out of your retirement plan, but DON'T!

Instead of you and the bank as parties to a demand account there are several parties to **your retirement account**. There may be up to four parties in your 401k plan:

- You are responsible for funding and managing the investments in **your retirement account.**

- The company you work for creates the plan specifics, participates in choosing the investments you can invest in, handles the internal paperwork, the money transfers, and matching contributions.

- The plan sponsor is the company that handles all the paperwork, accounting, legal issues and makes sure your investment dollars go where you want them. They are also responsible for reconciliation, creation and mailing of the quarterly statements and all the Ra-Ra propaganda that you get sent to your home. The plan sponsor charges you to perform all of these functions. Typically, insurance companies charge higher fees because they bundle your plan assets in an annuity. Annuities are usually the most expensive plan because they usually pay out the highest commissions to the salespeople. The money you pay the plan sponsor is deducted from your retirement account automatically and usually every month. You normally won't be shown that transaction on your statements.

- Investment companies are the companies that manage the mutual funds or other investments that are in **your retirement account**. The investment companies hire the investment managers who actually do the buying and selling of the investments and all the research to pick out those investments. You pay the investment company to manage the investments you invest in. The money you pay the investment company is deducted from your retirement account automatically and usually every month. You normally won't be shown that transaction on your statements.

Myth two: "I don't have any good choices to invest in." This may have been the case ten years ago, but several lawsuits and legal rulings have helped you in this area. Remember that investing is a very personal and intimate affair. You may have a favorite investment that you want included in the retirement plan. Ask your human resources department if it can be included. The worst thing that will happen is for them to say, "No." Usually additional investment options can't be added due to the laws that require certain investment categories that must be included, or the cost of adding a new investment option may be too expensive. The more investment options added to the 401k plan, the more it may cost your employer. However, you just might get what you asked for. Your employer will draw the line somewhere and say, "No more."

There are laws that tell the plan sponsor and employer that certain investment options have to be in the plan. The plan sponsor tells your employer what investment options are available and advises on how many investments in each category they recommend. I've put a few 401k plans together, and I can tell you the best investments are pretty easy to pick out of the available options. I've never sat down to build a retirement account where the employer says, "Can we choose some really bad investments. I want to screw over my employees." It's the employer who usually says, "Look, I want the best investment options available for my employees because I'm also going to be part of this retirement plan."

Myth three: "I don't know what my account is doing." At a minimum for a retirement account you should be receiving:

- Quarterly statements showing your account balances
- How much you contributed into **your retirement plan** that quarter
- How much your employer contributed to **your retirement plan**
- What investments you are invested in and in what percentage amounts
- Beginning value of **your retirement account**
- Ending value of **your retirement account**

This account statement should be printed by the plan sponsor and mailed to you by the plan sponsor. This is important because if there is any type of fraud or theft in **your retirement plan**, it will be detected on the statement. You will need to be diligent in reviewing **your retirement plan** statement. If you get a generic statement that doesn't come from the plan sponsor, it could mean that the company that is supposed to be managing your retirement plan isn't. The statement is the only proof you receive that this is **your retirement plan** and your money. If something looks wrong, either go to the human resources department where you work or call the free phone number and check it out. We are very lucky because of all of the laws and checks and balances this doesn't happen very often. When dealing with large sums of money some people will be tempted to steal from others. Don't make that an excuse not to participate in **your retirement plan.**

Most plan sponsors now offer Internet access to your retirement plan. Since most plan assets are in mutual funds that don't trade until the major markets close, your account values aren't updated until the evening. I usually tell people that if they really want to look at their accounts to see a one-day change, to do it in the mornings. I don't recommend daily tracking of any retirement account. It is just to frustrating seeing your account vary every day. Monthly or twice a monthly should be the most you look at the value of the account. If you want to see when transactions occur, that's a different story and transactions like deposits or withdrawals are OK to check daily.

Myth four: "Everyone else's retirement plan has better returns than mine."

The biggest myth about investing is really a Big Fat Lie! Everyone lies about the returns they get on their investments. Everyone else has a better plan. Everyone else gets more matching money. Everyone else has highflying investments. It's a constant, like death and taxes, everybody lies when it

176

comes to their investments.

The really good liars will mix in some facts and create a very convincing fairy tale. I have my nieces convinced that the squirrels around my apartment complex chase down small dogs. Then like a pack of piranha, they eat the small dogs in 30 seconds. All that's left are the bones and dog collar. Fact, I live in an apartment complex. Fact, there are squirrels that live there. A good story with a few facts thrown in, but obviously completely untrue. Just don't tell my nieces Camey and Crissey!

Since you will never show **your retirement plan** statement to anyone other than your investment advisor, performance has become a game of lies. Like any gambler who boasts about one giant win; every gambler has had one big win in their life. What isn't said is that it cost those same gamblers dearly in loses which that one big win didn't come close to covering.

Those same persons who lie about performance also won't tell you the name of their investment guru who made these unbelievable investment picks. That person doesn't want you looking up this investment guru so you can invest some of your money with that person. You may find out that this investment guru doesn't exist, or worse his returns aren't even close to what you were told. I have had to calm down more than one very good long-term investor who fell prey to these locker-room stories.

I know that many people carry over their mistrust of pension plans called 'Defined Benefit Plans'. In the defined benefit plan, the **benefits** you receive when you retired were defined by your employment. Usually, one week of your yearly salary is added to your retirement every year you work for the company. The longer you work, the more weeks' pay you are to receive per year when you retire. Also, along the same path, it is assumed that you will be making more money each year so your weekly earnings will also be worth more. The weekly earnings are added together over the term of your employment. The resulting accumulation is a set amount that is supposed to be guaranteed to you over the rest of your life.

The defined benefit plan is endangered and will be extinct in a few decades. With the life expectancy of the average worker increasing, this defined benefit plan has become a huge burden to many companies. No one had the foresight to predict the advances in medicine and how they would affect companies in this way. The company offering a defined benefit plan carries almost all the risks associated with a retirement plan. Some of the big risks are:

- Funding the retirement plan

- Investing those funds in the retirement plan in a manner to achieve the retirement needs of all participants in the retirement plan

- Taking all variables of human life into account to ensure that there is enough money in the plan now and in the future to meet all contractual obligations to the participants of the retirement plan

I'm not making a judgment on any of the parties who are part of a defined benefit plan. I think that all the parties in this type of a plan are the losers. I wish that I had some miracle way to save all these defined benefit plans from going bust, or a way to guarantee that people who are receiving a retirement income from them are going to continue to receive the same benefits for the rest of their lives. The trust that they placed in the company should count for something. The fact is that people are living longer, much longer than anyone anticipated, and there is no way that the defined benefit plans are going to be able to keep up.

The 401k plan is called a 'Defined Contribution Plan'. In a

defined contribution plan the **<u>contribution</u>** that the company makes is defined by the plan, not the benefits that you will receive. That doesn't sound very different, does it? Well it is very different! The big difference is **<u>who</u>** bears the most risk in **<u>your retirement plan</u>**. You are accepting almost all of the risk by participating in a 401k plan. That risk is huge and starts with:

- Funding **your retirement plan**

- Investing those funds in **your retirement plan** in such a manner as to achieve your retirement goals

- Ensuring that the company does contribute to **your retirement plan**

- Once retired and taking distribution from **your retirement plan**, taking only enough that is needed so as to not deplete your own retirement plan before your needs end.

Now, I don't know about you, but when I look at all that risk above as an investment professional, I see lots of RISK! Companies sponsoring a 401k plan really are getting a good deal here, but so are the participants. I'm really jazzed about this type of retirement plan. The participants, you, are given more control over your lives, and I like more control rather than less. I know there are people out there that are terrified by this, but hopefully with a little education and some experience, you can get excited about this too!

Now, hopefully we've cleared up most of your unrealistic concerns or myths because there are too many real concerns and risks that you do have to deal with. Remember, you and only you bear the risk and have the responsibility in a 401k to actively:

- Funding **<u>your retirement plan</u>**

- Investing the funds in **<u>your retirement plan</u>** in a manner to achieve your retirement goals

- Ensuring that the company contributes what they are obligated to into **your retirement plan**

- Reviewing into **your retirement plan** statements

- Once retired and taking distribution from **your retirement plan**, taking only enough that is needed so as to not deplete your own retirement plan before your needs end or the end is mandated by law.

FUNDING YOUR RETIREMENT PLAN

Why should you fund your own retirement plan? Because no one else is going to do it! Don't count on Social Security being around in its present form much longer. It was supposed to be a short-term measure during the Great Depression of 1929 and it wasn't designed to last this long. Think of Social Security as a defined benefit plan. Social Security has the same flaws built into a company-sponsored defined benefit plan and it just won't be around forever. Oh, I know the Federal Government has lots more money to throw into the Social Security program, and it may survive in some carved up form. Just don't count on Social Security to fund your basic retirement needs.

OK, so maybe you're getting the hint that you have to fund **your retirement plan**. Where do you start? How about enrolling in the plan 401k at your place of employment? I know that everyone doesn't have a plan at work so maybe it's time you asked for one. Typically, there should be some type of retirement plan where you work. Ask the human resources department for the forms and any information that is available on your company-sponsored 401k plan.

The plan sponsors of 401k plans want you to enroll in the plan. The more money you put into the plan, the more money the plan sponsors make. There should be lots and lots of FREE, easy to read information available. There may also be a FREE phone number to call where after a few presses of the buttons on your phone a live body will come on and discuss almost any questions you have about **your retirement plan**. Don't ask these people for investment advice. They can't give investment advice; you have to be licensed to give out investment advice.

These live bodies that you talk too on the FREE phone number can answer questions like how to fill out the forms you have. Take the time and then walk you through whatever you need to get your questions answered. They will hopefully add some information that you may not have known you needed to know. Like any call center, some of the people on the other end of the line are excellent and some are just waiting for their shift to end. Don't be afraid to ask for a specific person who you know will take the time to answer your questions in a way that things become perfectly clear. Well, perfectly clear as long as you're talking to them. Things tend to cloud up as soon as you hang up the phone, but that's natural. You can always call them back again!

You now have all the forms filled out except for the investment options. Let me tell you there are so many people who want to give you their opinion on this matter of where to invest your money. If they start by telling you how rich they got on one trade or how they beat the market, run away quickly. If they start out by asking you some intelligent questions like:

- When do you plan on retiring?

- What is your experience in investing?

- Have you set any investment goals?

- What was you favorite investment and why?

You may want to listen to what they have to say. I've said many times that investing is a very personal, intimate process. No two people look at investing in the same way. Get coaching or advice on investment matters and then you make the final decision.

Feel free to ask your family and close friends for their opinions. Some may be very helpful in determining what is important for you to look at or use as guidelines for investing. In the end it's all about you and what makes you feel anxious. Yes, I said 'anxious', not comfortable or secure. Investing is a nervous business. The only people I know who are comfortable are people with enough cash in the bank to retire immediately. There are very few of those people in the world.

You now have all the information filled out to enroll in the retirement plan where you work. How much should you take out of your hard-earned money and stick away in your retirement plan?

Your employer should offer some type of matching option in the 401k plan. I look at this in three ways. First, as an investment advisor I look at this like an immediate return on my investment. Let's say your employer offers to match 50% of 5% of your salary. That means if you contribute 5% of your pay into your retirement plan, they will add half of what you put in in cold hard cash! A 50% return on your investment! Man, life doesn't get any better than that. It's time to celebrate every payday! Making 50% return guaranteed should be illegal, but it's not.

Second, some of you see your retirement plan as gambling. How would you like to go to Las Vegas and sit down at the blackjack table? You lay down one dollar and get dealt two cards. No matter what the dealer draws you win every hand. The dealer hands over 50 cents and you tuck that $1.50 into a pocket in your jacket which is called **your retirement plan**. You take out another dollar, lay it on the table, you receive two cards and you win another 50 cents. Now, we're not talking about huge money until you realize that every payday you step up to this same blackjack table and you keep winning week after week, year after year.

Third, some of you feel underpaid and most of you probably are, I know that I'm underpaid. By contributing to **your retirement plan** it's like getting a raise. You are now making more money than you would be if you didn't contribute to your retirement plan. The company has to pay this money; it's in the contract of the plan. It's like taking the money right out of your employer's pocket and shaking it in their face. Their hands are tied because they have to give the money to you. You beat THE MAN at his own game! Even the people who are THE MAN are beating themselves when they participate.

So to answer the question, how much do you invest in your retirement plan? The first part of the answer is the minimum amount to get all of this free money available in **your retirement plan** as you can! You deserve a raise or to beat the house every payday, and this is one way to do it. You also deserve to pay yourself for the hard work you do. You can do this by funding **your retirement plan**.

You have started out with the minimum amount to get all this free money. No one is going to call you into their office and say, "We've looked at **your retirement plan** and we think you should add more in contributions or increase the risk level." By participating in the 401k plan **you have borne those risks** and you need to proactively adjust up the amount of funding to **your retirement plan**.

The second part of the answer is that you will also need to bump up the amount you contribute to **your retirement plan** over the years. As you receive a raise in your pay where you work, you need to raise the amount you put into your retirement plan. Some companies allow you to receive a bonus or profit sharing either as a one-time check or a depositor into your retirement account. You know what I'm going to say, put it in your retirement account. I know it hurts to see your money locked up in your retirement plan, but it will taste so sweet when you retire and you get to do the things that you really want.

INVESTING THE FUNDS IN YOUR RETIREMENT PLAN IN A MANNER TO ACHIEVE YOUR RETIREMENT GOALS

This is the hardest part of **your retirement plan**. This investment area is where your needs and goals are factored in and these two variables are perpetually changing. Some things that make your needs change:

- You get married

- You have children

- You decide to go back to school

- You decide to retire early or late

   Some things that make your goals change:

- You decide on an RV as a second retirement home

- You decide to open a small business when you retire to keep yourself busy

- You decide to take up an expensive hobby when you retire

- You decide that you want to travel for two years and see all the places that have interested you or you have read about your whole life

These changes to your needs and goals are a natural part of

living life. All of the investment-return questions can be answered by defining a time line and a little simple math. What you won't want to see is the answer that you get back from the simple math. It will tell you that:

1. You haven't saved enough to retire in the manner that you would like to.

2. The returns on **your retirement plan** assets are far below what you need to retire in the manner that you would like to.

Don't get depressed, well OK, get a little depressed. Then do something! Like rereading the chapter in this book on asset allocation and regularly adding more money to **your retirement plan**.

401k plans aren't known for having a huge amount of investment options. What they have to have by law is investment options in several categories. You need to research the investment options in your retirement plan to:

- Pick which investments in **your retirement plan** are best for you.

- Pick which investments in **your retirement plan** work with your current asset allocation.

HOW TO PICK OUT THE BEST INVESTMENTS OPTIONS IN YOUR RETIREMENT PLAN

Since the number of investments inside **your retirement plan** is limited this is a pretty easy process to describe and go through. You need a few things. First a list of all of the investment options available in **your retirement plan**. The best list to have has all the investment options listed, the returns for each option listing one, three, five and ten-year returns and lists the investment options by categories like:

- Money market

- Fixed income

- Domestic large cap equity

- Domestic mid cap equity

- Domestic small cap equity

- International equity

With that paper in hand you now need to get onto the Internet and go to:

www.morninstar.com

The four key points I look at when investing in a retirement plan with a limited number of investments are:

- Manager tenure

- Morningstar style box location

- Beta

- Internal fees

Manager tenure is very important to me. I like to give the mutual fund manager the credit when it is due and if they have been managing a fund for three years, I take a big black sharpie marker and write overall return numbers greater than three years. The only exception, remember this is Wall Street and there are always exceptions, is for an index fund where the manager really doesn't pick the investments.

The Morningstar 3-by-3 style box is next important to me. The name of the fund tells me what my money should be invested in, such as: large-cap, international or government bonds. The style box shows me where my money is invested. You see, mutual fund managers have lots of wiggle room when buying investments in the mutual funds they manage. A mutual fund manager of a large cap value fund may have more dollars invested in growth and a good portion in mid-cap. The mutual fund is no longer a large-cap value but a multilevel growth fund. Oh, it's all legal. The prospectus which you received when you invested in the fund contained all the nasty little details, but you probably couldn't understand it past the first few lines so in the garbage it went. That's why the style box works so well, no lies, no smoke, and no mirrors.

Beta is another important measure.

Beta (finance)

From Wikipedia, the free encyclopedia

"The Beta coefficient, in terms of finance and investing, is a measure of volatility of a stock or portfolio in relation to the rest of the financial market."

An asset with a beta of 0 means that its price is not at all correlated with the market; that asset is independent. A positive beta means that the asset generally follows the market. A negative beta shows that the asset inversely follows the market; the asset generally decreases in value if the market goes up.

A beta of 1 means that the investment will move almost exactly with the market. The market goes up 5% and this investment should go up 5%. A beta of 2 means that this investment goes up twice what the market does. In good times a market move of 5% upward will move this investment up 10%. If the market moves 3% down this investment should go down 6%. A .5 beta means that this investment will move one half the direction of the market. A 4% move will move your investment 2%. A negative beta indicates that if the market goes up this investment will go down.

- You want an investment with a high beta in an up market.

- You want a low beta in a down market

Internal fees charged by the mutual fund are the final important item I look at. Higher fees attached to a mutual fund or ETF equate to lower returns. You should expect to pay more in fees for international investments because of the huge distance that needs to be covered and various currencies used.

WHAT IS YOUR CURRENT ASSET ALLOCATION

If you don't have an asset allocation selected for you, go back to the chapter on that and create one. It's not that hard and once you go through the drill a few times it will become easy and fun. Well, easy at least, I really like that part in a geeky investment nerdy sort of way. Keep in mind that asset allocation is as much art as science. If it looks good and feels good, then go with it. Otherwise revise the asset allocation until it both looks good and feels good.

Once you have your asset allocation determined, now is the time to decide the best investments you have available in each asset class and each account. You need to look at all of your accounts as one for asset allocation purposes. Then divvy out the money in each account to the best investments available. Don't be worried that one account has all the international investments and another has only fixed income. Asset allocation is all about the percentage of your assets in different asset classes, not where those assets are located.

BIG CONCEPT

Your retirement plan is tax exempt so when you buy or sell in this account taxes aren't an issue. You should then place your most tax inefficient 'aggressive' investments here. That would be equities in general. If you have a taxable account like a bank account or some type of brokerage account, think fixed income here first; these investments are

usually held to maturity or traded less. The more traded and taxed investments are bought and sold more often.

Here's a quick example of how I go through the entire process. For simplicity the client has one large 401k account:

1. Determine the client's asset allocation.

2. Determine the best investments in all the asset classes in this retirement plan.

3. Pick the investments for each asset class.

4. Calculate the asset allocation of my picks. This one needs an explanation. I like to use the S&P 500 index fund if available in a retirement account. This index holds large, mid and small-cap investments in both value and growth. It is what I like to call a core holding, and I will build off of it. I usually allocate a large portion, about 40% of the account, to international so I like to use at least two investment choices here.

5. Readjust investments to meet clients' asset allocation.

ENSURING THAT THE COMPANY CONTRIBUTES WHAT THEY ARE OBLIGATED TO INTO YOUR OWN RETIREMENT PLAN

This is one of the easiest checks you can do on **your retirement plan**. On your quarterly statement there are several sections. Quarterly statements are designed to give lots of information and are usually in a sectional format. Sections that are common are: name and address, employer information, account balances, investments and performance. The layout of the statements change quite a bit from plan sponsor to plan sponsor, but the information is usually the same. One of these sections should list the contributions from outside sources, i.e. you and your employer.

First, make sure that all the money taken out of your paycheck has been put into **your retirement plan**. Like I said earlier, there may be a slight time delay in the money getting into **your retirement plan**. Anything that doesn't look right requires a call to the plan sponsors free telephone number to check on. Remember that this is a summary statement; you may be able to get a more detailed statement if you ask.

Second, make sure that the correct employer match to **your retirement plan** makes it to your account. The same area on your quarterly statement that lists your contributions should also list your employer's contribution. Now every 401k plan is slightly different when it comes to employer match. I recommend that you take your statement to the human resources department and review the entire document together. You can also use the free phone number and go over your statement with someone at that phone number. Your statement is usually imaged on their computer system so the person talking to you on the phone can retrieve a copy of so they can go over it with you, line by line.

To determine the correct employer matching contribution, you will need to know exactly what the employer should put in as a match. This is normally stated in a grammatical form and not numeric so it's your job to convert it. I'll do a quick example:

Employer match is 50% of your contribution, up to maximum of 5% of your present salary.

Your present yearly salary =$35,000

$35,000 X .05 (maximum matching amount 5%=.05) = $1,750.00

$1,750 X .50 (employer match 50% = .50) = $875.00

You get paid twice a month, on the 1st and 15th

Your paycheck = $35,000 / 24 =$1,458.33

$1,458.33 X .05 = $72.91 (the max you can put in and receive the matching contribution)

$72.91 X .50 = $36.46 (the maximum amount of the matching contribution)

One last thought on employer contributions. Most plans have a 'vesting schedule' for employer contributions. This means that the money the employer puts into your account isn't really yours until some time in the future. It could be one year, two years, three years or longer. The employer uses this vesting schedule as a way to try to keep an employee for a minimum amount of time. If you're stuck in a bad job, don't worry about this money. Get out of there! No amount of money is worth staying in a bad job!

ONCE RETIRED AND TAKING DISTRIBUTIONS FROM YOUR RETIREMENT PLAN, TAKE ONLY ENOUGH THAT IS NEEDED SO AS TO NOT DEPLETE YOUR OWN RETIREMENT PLAN BEFORE YOUR NEEDS END

OK, here's where we get into some really detailed formulas and fuzzy science, NOT!

I let the math majors and PhD's in finance do the work for me.

6%

That's the magic number. That's what all the finance wizards have agreed upon that you can take out of your conservatively allocated portfolio and still maintain the value of your portfolio over a long period of time. The value of your portfolio will fluctuate some with the changing economic and interest rate environments, but it should average out around the same number so long as you stick to taking out only 6% per year.

- That means that you have a 'conservatively allocated' portfolio – roughly 80% fixed income and 20% large-cap equities.

- That means that you still actively manage the portfolio!

- That means that you still rebalance the portfolio at regular intervals!

- That means you reinvest dividends back into the portfolio!

- That means that you take 6% and only 6% of the total value of the portfolio!

An example is in order I feel:

$100,000 X .06 (.06 = 6%) = $6,000

That means that for every $100,000 you save for retirement, you can expect to take out $6,000 and keep the principal value intact. That's a strong case to save twice what you think you should in **your retirement plan**. That is also a strong case to get started saving right NOW!

It is not an excuse to say, "I'll never be able to save enough, so I just won't do anything." It's never too late to start saving! It's never too late to start taking control of your finances! Saving and being financially disciplined is not easy and it's not glamorous. It is a fact of our lives and the sooner we take control, the sooner we will feel more in control of our lives, and that feeling is good and comforting.

SET UP A SCHEDULE AND ROUTINE TO REVIEW YOUR RETIREMENT PLAN

You should put some type of simple system together to speed up the quarterly review process:

- Have a folder easily available in your house to put all the literature and statements into as you receive them in the mail. Go through all the papers in this folder every time you receive a quarterly statement for **your retirement plan**.

- When the Federal Open Market Committee changes the direction of interest rates, you will need to change your asset allocation in **your retirement plan**.

- When you get a raise, you need to increase your contributions into **your retirement plan**.

- When you get a bonus, put some of it into **your retirement plan**.

- At the end of the year, review your asset allocation.

This process should take no more than five minutes at the end of each quarter and fifteen minutes at year-end. Time well spent indeed!

Commonsense stuff you need to remind yourself every month:

- Your account won't go up every month/quarter/year.

- Think long-term when making any big decisions.

- Don't deviate from your asset allocation on a spur of the moment decision. Sleep on all big decisions.

- Doing the right thing is often very scary.

- Hug your children and spouse, tell them you love them and are proud of them.

CONCLUSION

This part is probably going to get me in some type of trouble. I have general asset allocation models that I use to start the asset allocation process. Whenever I look at a new account that I will be managing, I have to start somewhere. The first step in any process is always the hardest so I have made this to make getting started easier. These are just starting points! Lots more work will be needed to these general asset allocation models to get them to fit for you.

LONG-TERM INVESTOR

Think long-term!

Save twice what you think you will need.

It's never too late to start saving.

Every time you get a raise…increase your payroll deduction for your 401k retirement plan.

'Home Equity loans' are really second mortgages. They make tons of money for the banks and other lending institutions at your expense. DO NOT TAKE ON ANY UNNEEDED DEBT!

Enjoy the journey of life and have fun!

Rising interest rate general asset allocation model for long-term investor

	CONSERVATIVE	AGGRESSIVE
FIXED INCOME	**30%**	**0%**
1 YEAR TO MATURITY	30%	
2 TO 5 YEARS TO MATURITY		
5 TO 10 YEARS TO MATURITY		
10 TO 30 YEARS TO MATURITY		
30-YEAR ZERO-COUPON BONDS		
EQUITY	**70%**	**100%**
LARGE-CAP VALUE	20%	15%
LARGE-CAP GROWTH	20%	15%
MID-CAP VALUE	5%	10%
MID-CAP GROWTH	5%	10%
SMALL-CAP VALUE	5%	5%
SMALL-CAP GROWTH	5%	5%
INTERNATIONAL	10%	40%

Lowering interest rate general asset allocation model for long-term investor

	CONSERVATIVE	AGGRESSIVE
FIXED INCOME	**65%**	**50%**
1 YEAR TO MATURITY		
2 TO 5 YEARS TO MATURITY		
5 TO 10 YEARS TO MATURITY		
10 TO 30 YEARS TO MATURITY		
30-YEAR ZERO-COUPON BONDS	65%	50%
EQUITY	**35%**	**50%**
LARGE-CAP VALUE	15%	10%
LARGE-CAP GROWTH	10%	10%
MID-CAP VALUE		5%
MID-CAP GROWTH		5%
SMALL-CAP VALUE		0%
SMALL-CAP GROWTH	10%	0%
INTERNATIONAL	15%	20%

TRANSITIONAL INVESTOR

Use changes in the direction of interest rate to reposition your asset allocation.

SAVE!!! SAVE!!! SAVE!!!!

Start planning for retirement and have fun!

Rising interest rate general asset allocation model for the transitional investor

	CONSERVATIVE	AGGRESSIVE
FIXED INCOME	**50%**	**30%**
1 YEAR TO MATURITY	25%	15%
2 TO 5 YEARS TO MATURITY	25%	15%
5 TO 10 YEARS TO MATURITY		
10 TO 30 YEARS TO MATURITY		
30-YEAR ZERO-COUPON BONDS		
EQUITY	**50%**	**70%**
LARGE-CAP VALUE	15%	20%
LARGE-CAP GROWTH	10%	15%
MID-CAP VALUE	5%	5%
MID-CAP GROWTH		5%
SMALL-CAP VALUE	5%	5%
SMALL-CAP GROWTH		5%
INTERNATIONAL	15%	15%

Lowering interest rate general asset allocation model for the transitional investor

	CONSERVATIVE	AGGRESSIVE
FIXED INCOME	**75%**	**50%**
1 YEAR TO MATURITY		
2 TO 5 YEARS TO MATURITY		
5 TO 10 YEARS TO MATURITY		
10 TO 30 YEARS TO MATURITY	50%	
30-YEAR ZERO-COUPON BONDS	25%	50%

EQUITY	25%	50%
LARGE-CAP VALUE	10%	15%
LARGE-CAP GROWTH	10%	15%
MID-CAP VALUE		5%
MID-CAP GROWTH		
SMALL-CAP VALUE		5%
SMALL-CAP GROWTH		
INTERNATIONAL	5%	10%

INCOME AND GROWTH INVESTORS

Watch your bond maturities!

Watch your bond call features!

Give something back to society!

Enjoy your retirement and have fun!

Rising interest rate general asset allocation model for the income and growth investor

	CONSERVATIVE	AGGRESSIVE
FIXED INCOME	85%	70%
1 YEAR TO MATURITY		
2 TO 5 YEARS TO MATURITY		
5 TO 10 YEARS TO MATURITY		
10 TO 30 YEARS TO MATURITY	85%	70%
30-YEAR ZERO-COUPON BONDS		
EQUITY	15%	30%
LARGE-CAP VALUE	10%	10%
LARGE-CAP GROWTH	5%	10%
MID-CAP VALUE		5%
MID-CAP GROWTH		
SMALL-CAP VALUE		5%
SMALL-CAP GROWTH		
INTERNATIONAL		

Lowering interest rate general asset allocation model for the income and growth investor

	CONSERVATIVE	AGGRESSIVE
FIXED INCOME	**85%**	**80%**
1 YEAR TO MATURITY		
2 TO 5 YEARS TO MATURITY		
5 TO 10 YEARS TO MATURITY		
10 TO 30 YEARS TO MATURITY	55%	50%
30-YEAR ZERO-COUPON BONDS	20%	20%
EQUITY	**15%**	**20%**
LARGE-CAP VALUE	10%	5%
LARGE-CAP GROWTH	5%	5%
MID-CAP VALUE		5%
MID-CAP GROWTH		
SMALL-CAP VALUE		5%
SMALL-CAP GROWTH	5%	
INTERNATIONAL	15%	

THINGS THAT I HAVE LEARNED ON WALL STREET ABOUT WEALTH

Since I have mainly dealt with high net worth individuals, I can tell you a few things about them.

People who get rich quick usually then get poor quick.

Very few people with money are able to relax and enjoy it. Most are emotionally burdened as their wealth increases.

Adults work too hard making money to enjoy life. When they have finally saved enough money to retire, they can't enjoy it the way they want to because they are too old to do the things they put off doing to make money.

Once people perceive that they have wealth, they then become obsessed with keeping that wealth. They develop a mentality that 'everyone is out to get their fortune'. That is partially true of family members, but not society in general.

Once a wealthy person has a major illness they become a basket case. They finally see death and seem to want to spend all of their wealth to stay alive. If they only had spent a little time along the journey of life to take care of their body so that it would last as long as their wealth.

Chapter 9

DIFFERENT WAYS TO PLACE AN EQUITY BUY OR SELL ORDER

This part of the book is definitely going to make you and save you money. I know from personal experience that most people haven't the foggiest idea of how many different configurations there are in an individual stock transaction. Most don't know that it's possible to first sell a stock, and then buy it back; it's called a short sale. How many of you know you can borrow money using your present portfolio as collateral to make an equity purchase? It's called 'margin', but it's not an investment strategy I use. That's because when you use margin you add leverage to the portfolio which can either dramatically increase your gains or your losses. I'm getting ahead of myself. Let's look at how to intelligently buy and sell a security.

An individual stock trade order needs to be in 'good order' or it will be rejected from trading. The trade order has to contain the minimum amount of required information. The required information for a trade is:

- The date the order was placed

- The time the order was placed

- The type of transaction (buy or sell) (long or short)

- The quantity of shares to trade

- The security symbol or CUSIP of the investment being traded

- Was the trade was solicited or unsolicited

- Will you accept the current price for the transaction ('at the market') or will you specify the price you want ('limit amount')

- What is the time frame you want this order to remain actively available to trade

- The name on the account being traded

- The account number on the account being traded

- The custodian firm holding the security

With all of this different information available to manipulate to meet your specific needs, the order ticket is a powerful tool. If you learn how the trade process works, you can use the process to be more specific on how you trade. Knowledge is power. The knowledgeable investor will make more money. The knowledgeable investor will also defend against taking huge loses on an investment. You will have to assume more responsibility as you make more detailed trade orders. As an experienced trader, the number-one reason for me making a trade error was that I was being rushed. Making a trade error usually means the trade is rejected or cancelled. It could also delay you getting into the queue to get your order filled. Take your time as you place your order; double and triple check your trade information. Let's take a look at each area of the trade order.

DATE/TIME

The date and time information is important to prove that you at some certain time have actually placed an order. If there is ever a dispute between you and the firm responsible for executing the trade, this may be a critical piece of information in resolving the problem. Trades can happen in an instant after entering them on the electronic system. What happens if they don't? Your order is lost in the process or slowed down. It could mean that you paid too much for your purchase or didn't receive enough for your sale. The date/time information is normally entered for you when you do an online trade or by the person who takes your order over the phone. When I worked for Dean Witter I would write up a paper 'Trade Ticket'. Then I turned the trade ticket in to the personnel in the 'Wire Room'. The first thing they would do is to timestamp the order with the same sort of time clock hourly workers would clock into work with. These people were responsible next for entering the orders into the computer system.

Individual stocks have a nasty habit of very abrupt price movement. This seems especially true when you are about to trade them. The time on your order is the proof that your order was in the queue at this moment in time. You can match the time on your confirmation with the daily price movement of the security and see if the price at that time corresponds with the price you bought at or sold at. It will never be to the penny of the current quoted market price due to the time lag for the quoting system. Usually on a highly traded stock the difference should be no more than a nickel or dime. If it's off by more than the difference between the bid and ask spread, you may have cause to contact the person or firm you traded through and ask for an explanation.

I have had only a few experiences where time was a factor in trading. Fidelity Investments, the firm my Registered Investment Advisory (RIA) business used to custody and trade for my clients accounts, has been very thorough and fair every time a trade problem had arisen. They researched my perceived problem and promptly gotten back to me with what they had determined. By the amount of information they have been able to discuss with me, I have always been comfortable with their decision no matter who is at fault. Sometimes the error was my fault and I accepted the blame. On the times that they did admit to an error, they have adjusted the trade to occur in the time frame disputed and the client didn't financially suffer in the trade.

Mutual Service Corp. was the broker/dealer we used when I worked at the insurance company. Mutual Service Corp. had a very different policy. First their policy was 'guilty until you prove your innocence'. Second, if the trade error made money, they would keep it. If the trade error lost money, you as the trader had to pay out of your own pocket for the trade error amount to make the client 'whole'.

In Wall Street terms 'being made whole' is adjusting the account to reflect what the trade would have looked like if there hadn't been a problem. That's another reason to carefully look over every confirmation and piece of paper you get from your finance people. Computer systems and people can and do make mistakes. If you bring the mistake to their attention, it is within their power to research it and fix any problem they find.

BUY/SELL

BUY LONG/SELL LONG

This is the typical type of trade that takes place for most investors. When you buy an equity long, it means that you are using a 'buy, hold then sell' strategy. First you buy a stock, you are now 'long' that company or position, you hold that position for some period of time, and then you sell the position, 'close your position'. In the 'buy long then sell long' scenario the investor believes that the investment they have just purchased will go up in value. It's a plain vanilla 'Buy Low-Sell High' strategy.

The following is an example of this. In January you would buy 100 shares of an individual equity you don't own in your investment account, say CAT (Caterpillar). Since you don't own that position in your investment account it is said by experienced investors that you have just 'opened a position in CAT'. Now you 'have a position in CAT' or 'I'm long CAT'. If you were to buy more shares of CAT before you sold all the shares you have 'added to your position in CAT'. But in July you sell all your shares of CAT or 'closed your position in CAT'.

The cash flows for a 'buy long/sell long' is that you pay money out of your wallet on the buy long transaction, a negative cash flow. You then receive any dividends paid by the position while you own the stock, a positive cash flow. Finally, you receive money back on the long sale transaction, a positive cash flow. The amount you pay on the long buy is the execution price multiplied by the number of shares plus the commission and any other fees, like an SEC fee. The amount you receive on the long sale is the number of shares times the execution price minus the commissions and fees.

While you own the stock you should receive all dividends that the company pays. You will need to pay attention to the two important dates associated with dividends. The first is the 'owner of record' date; this is the date that everyone who owns the stock at the close of business will be entitled to the dividend. The transfer agent is responsible for knowing at the end of every trading day who owns stock in the company and how many shares they own. The price of an investment will usually adjust down immediately after the dividend is paid, usually by the amount of the dividend. This is very important if you have a limit order placed on this investment.

The second important date is the 'payable date' which is the day that the money will be transferred into your brokerage account or mailed to you in the form of a check. If you sell the stock between the 'owner of record date' and 'payable date' you will still receive the dividend.

SELL SHORT/ BUY SHORT

What if you believe that a stock is way over valued and you expect the price to come down? Can you make any money in this scenario? The answer is yes. Instead of the sequence of buy **long** low then sell **long** high, you can sell **short** high then buy **short** low. When you sell short you believe that the position will go down in value. It's a 'sell, hold then buy' strategy. I know it's a little weird, but it does work in practice.

The trade ticket you fill out online may have 'buy' and 'sell' in one box and 'long' or 'short' in another box. They may all be combined 'buy', 'sell' 'buy short', 'sell short' in the same box. Be sure to spend time looking over all of the options in the pull down boxes. You will run across 'option' with 'open' and 'close'. Option trading is the subject for another more advanced book; let's just work on the basics first.

Here's an example. You believe that WMT (Walmart) has had a strong run up over the past few months and it's time for the price of the stock to fall or pullback. You sell short 100 shares of WMT in March. You have just 'sold short WMT', 'shorted WMT', or, 'I'm short WMT'. So now it's June and you are ready to buy short or 'close my short position', or 'cover my short'. You will buy short 100 shares of WMT; you have now closed your short position in WMT.

What really happened when you sold short WMT was that you borrowed 100 shares from someone who is long 100 shares of WMT. Then you sold those borrowed shares. The person who has loaned you those shares will probably never know. You are now responsible for paying the owner of those shares you borrowed all dividends that any stockowner would have received from Walmart. See, you sold his shares, but the long owner is still entitled to the ownership rights so you have to pay dividends out of your pocket to the owner. This is another one of the weird rules with selling short.

The cash flows for a short sale are that you receive the money in your investment account for the sale short proceeds, a positive cash flow. Remember on a sale transaction that money comes into your wallet. As long as you have the open short position the sale proceeds money MUST stay in your account.

You then have to hold the short sale position for some amount of time. If the company you sold short pays a dividend, you will need to pay the long owner of the position you sold that same amount out of your investment account, a negative cash flow. When you buy short, to close the short position, you will pay first out of the money received on the short sale, a negative cash flow. Any money remaining will be released into your investment account and you have made a profit. If the trade is a losing trade, then the balance of the funds for the short buy will come out of your account to cover the loss.

In the 'sell short then buy short' scenario the investor believes that the stock they have just sold will go down in value. It's a pure and simple 'Sell High-Buy low' strategy.

MARKET/ LIMIT

As an investor you get to choose what price you are willing to pay for most of your investment transactions. If you were willing to accept the current trading price for your investment transaction, you would choose a 'market order'. This is an order to execute immediately at the current market price 'where the market is at'. This is the way most orders are executed and the trade usually happens very fast. Use a market order when you definitely want this position right now, price is a secondary concern.

A 'limit order' is a powerful tool and I use it on most of the trades I enter. It sets a maximum price you are willing to pay for a security on the buy side, or a minimum price you are willing to receive on the sell side. I know the basic price movements of all of the securities I have purchased for my clients' accounts. If I believe that I can get the security at 5.0% less or even 2% less and time is no issue, I will place the order with a limit on it. I believe that it shows my clients that I am working hard for them to squeeze out ever last penny in savings to create more investment return. This is not a hard strategy to learn, but it does have some downsides.

One of the downsides is that if you really wanted this security but just couldn't pay the market price, you may never own it. I had this happen to me with CAT (Caterpillar). I wanted to put this security into a few accounts. The price had come down to around $35. I put in an order at $34, but the stock went up to $38 and I didn't get it. I upped the limit to $35 and the stock went to $45. CAT is now trading around $70 a share and I still want to own it in a few portfolios. The trick with limit orders is asking yourself one simple question: "How bad do I want to own CAT?" I want CAT in my clients' portfolios but not bad enough to pay the market price. I can't tell you what price I would buy it at, however, but when it gets to that price, I will know it.

A limit order will expire at some time, and you need to know exactly when your limit orders do expire. Usually active or open limit orders are listed on your monthly or quarterly statements. This is another good reason to always review these statements thoroughly.

On the sell side I use limit orders for when I purchase a

security and have a definite selling price in mind. I may buy a security with the expectation that it will go up $2 and then come back down. I enter a sell limit order on the sell price I think the stock will rise to and then sit and watch. If I change my mind, I can always cancel the limit order.

It doesn't cost anything to place or cancel a trade order. Some brokerages may charge more in commissions for a limit order, but as more and more firms offer online trading those charges are disappearing. You are taking the time to read this, take the time when you place an order and use this knowledge to save some money.

STOP-LOSS

A 'stop-loss' is a defensive tool used to either lock in gains or lessen your losses. Most people never use this tool and it has really hurt them in the wallet. It's simple, easy and most of the professional traders use it, so why not you? A stop-loss order is used only for the equity positions you already own. It is a sell order that sits dormant on the trading desk or floor of the exchange until either the security drops down to that price specified on the order ticket, you cancel the stop-loss order, or it expires.

The time an order expires may vary from firm to firm. When you place a stop-loss order, it should be stated on the trade confirmation how long the order will be in force, or when it will expire. You are responsible for monitoring this feature. All stop-loss orders should be listed on your monthly or quarterly statements as an 'open order' somewhere.

Let's look at an example of how this stop-loss order works. You buy 100 shares of Florida Power and Light (FPL) at $40. It's the beginning of June and the start of hurricane season in Florida, the main market for this company. Forecasters have predicted an unusually heavy hurricane season this year. You like the company and the nice dividend so you are reluctant to sell. You don't, however, want to lose your shirt in the case of a disaster so you decide to place a stop-loss order on this security. By looking at the previous year's chart of the price movement of FPL you see that the stock price may drop $4 just before a hurricane hits Florida. Since you want to keep this security, unless it really losses its value, you will place the stop-loss at $35.00 below the current price of $40.

So it's now September and a hurricane approaches Florida. There may have been a hurricane in August and investors are nervous. The price gets close to $35 and on one particular heavy day of trading the price does drop below $35, say $34.90. Your stop-loss order now instantly becomes a 'sell order at the market'. Your order will queue up with all the current market orders and you will get the price of FPL at the time you order executes. It could be more or less than the $35, but it will be at the current market price.

Another scenario, it's still September and a hurricane approaches Florida. There may have been a hurricane in August and investors are nervous. The price gets close to $35 but never goes under $35 for the rest of the year. You still own FPL and your stop-loss order will eventually expire.

Using limit orders and stop-loss orders are easy and an acceptable strategy if you spend the time to research the security that you will use it on. Don't expect your stockbroker to do that for you because this just doesn't make them any money. It will make you money or save you money, so spend a little time and energy. There are plenty of short articles that spell out the basics of these strategies.

One other important use of these stop-loss orders is when you are on vacation or unreachable by your stockbroker by phone. If he doesn't have authorization to trade in your account without your permission, you could really get screwed if a huge market sell off occurred and you can't be reached to approve a few transactions. Just something to think about...

THE TIME FRAME AN ORDER WILL REMAIN OPEN

Most orders submitted to the exchanges for equities are 'market' orders. That means that you are willing to pay or receive whatever the current price set by the market for the security you want to trade is. The order is entered and is routed through the computer system, someone on the other side of the trade is found and your order is 'filled' or 'executed'. This happens in a matter of seconds. For most people this is just fine, but for me, I've learned how to play the system a little.

DAY – GOOD TILL CANCEL

Day or Good-Till-Cancelled (GTC) on an order specifies the amount of time you want your order to be available for trading. A 'day' order will only be authorized for trading until the end of today's current trading activity. If the order was not filled, than it will be automatically cancelled and deleted from the trading systems. Most market orders are placed as day orders because they usually execute in a couple of minutes. If you ever watch CNBC right at four p.m. the paper that the traders on the floor of the NYSE are throwing up into the air were their day orders that didn't fill and are now worthless.

Good-Till-Cancelled (GTC) orders are a powerful tool for investors. A 'market' order can't be a GTC order because market orders fill immediately at the market price. When you place a GTC order, you need to specify a 'limit', the minimum/maximum price your trade will execute at and how long you are willing to wait for that price. Now a GTC order is a two-edge sword. It can get you a better price by waiting a while and buying on a dip or it can leave you stranded watching the price go up, up, up and you not owning the position.

I use GTC orders for anticipated price movements over a longer time frame. I have it in my head exactly what price I want to pay for a stock. I don't always know how I arrive at that price, but it is a set price, if I pay more than that price, I feel as though I've paid too much. For a stock like this I set a limit price at what I would pay and enter the order as a GTC. I now sit back and wait. If the price of the stock goes down, I have purchased it at my price. If the price stays where it is or goes up, that's OK too. All Good-Till-Cancelled (GTC) orders should be listed on your monthly or quarterly statements as an "open order" somewhere.

For a stock I want to own at the current price. I know the price movement because I usually watch a stock for several months before buying. I know the average daily range it will move in price. I take that range and subtract it from the current price and enter in a limit order for the DAY. Yes, only for the day. Here's my thinking. Some trader now has my puny little order for 300 shares of some stock sitting on his desk. It's a few pennies away from the market. The trader doesn't get paid on expired orders so magically my order gets filled at the price I set. This is a simple strategy to make or save money, and it works.

Why fight over a few cents per share? If I trade 500 shares and I shave ten cents a share off the price, I save $50.00. The trade cost me $25 or less. I'm already ahead by $25 on that investment or I have just saved my client some money. I feel good. For one brief nanosecond I controlled that huge financial empire called Wall Street. That was a winning trade! If you do that day/limit order one time, you've paid for this book. Make it part of your investing regiment and you are a more profitable investor!

Most brokerage firms have a time limit on how long they will keep a GTC order open, which is normally three to six months. I know that when I was getting my securities licenses GTC orders were automatically cancelled on two set dates per year by the exchanges. So if you place a GTC order, find out when your GTC order expires and write down that date somewhere.

FILL OR KILL

Instead of a GTC order you can use a Fill or Kill. This restriction requires that the order you just placed is immediately completed in its entirety or cancelled. You would use this on an equity that has a very volatile price movement and you want the price it is trading at right now. This can also be used for a thinly traded, illiquid equity to help push the trade through. I have never used this restriction on any trades I have entered.

IMMEDIATE OR CANCEL

This restriction requires that this order is immediately filled at the bid or offer price you have specified. All or only a portion of the order may be executed. Any portion of the order not immediately filled is cancelled. You want this equity now, but at your price. I have never used this restriction on any trades I have entered.

ON THE OPEN

This will be on a 'best effort' by the trader to get your order filled at the opening of the market that your security is traded on. I have never used this, but the traders I talk to say that they work hard to get the order filled in the first fifteen minutes of trading.

ON THE CLOSE

This will be on a 'best effort' by the trader to get your order filled at the close of the market that your security is traded on.

Traders start to work these orders in the last fifteen minutes before trading is halted. I have never used this restriction on any trades I have entered.

ALL OR NONE

A condition placed on an order indicating that the entire order be filled or no part of it. I have had large limit orders partially execute over several days. Each partial execution carries a full trade commission, so I paid three different commissions to get the order filled. After that fiasco I started using all or none on all my limit orders.

DO NOT REDUCE

This prevents a limit order price or stop-loss price from being reduced by the amount of the dividend when a stock goes ex-dividend. Ex-dividend date is another term for 'holder of record' date. A limit order's price will automatically be lowered by the amount of the dividend unless this is added to the order. I use this when I want to buy the stock but want to wait until the dividend is paid, usually for tax purposes.

The stock's price is reduced after a stock split. The use of a 'do not reduce' on an order will also prevent the price on your limit order from adjusting for the split price. If you own 100 shares in a stock with a current price of $60 per share, you have a limit order to sell those 100 shares at $65. The stock splits two for one. You now have twice as many shares, 200 shares, worth half the dollar value, $30 each share. Overall the total dollar value of the investment is still the same. A hundred shares times $60= $6000= 200 shares times $30. Your limit order with a 'do not reduce' on it remains to sell 100 shares at $65. Without a 'do not reduce' it would change to sell 200 shares at $32.50.

QUANTITY

Quantity is the amount in number of shares of stock you want to trade. For stocks it's pretty simple, if you want 100 ownership shares in a company, you buy 100 shares of stock. You will pay the execution price times the number of shares plus commission costs for a buy transaction. For a sale transaction you will get the execution price times the number of shares minus commissions.

SECURITY SYMBOL OR CUSIP

The security symbol or CUSIP (Committee on Uniform Security Identification Procedures) defines what specific security this transaction centers around. If it is a stock, then it will have a unique one, two, three, or four-letter symbol and a CUSIP, for example, F for Ford Motor Co., BA for Boeing, CAT for Caterpillar and MSFT for Microsoft. This will normally be all that you will need to trade an equity. Some equities have several different classes of shares, mostly non-voting shares which require a '.' and letter of the share class to follow the symbol; Berkshire Hathaway has an 'A' (BRK.A) and B (BRK.B) class shares. You would have to specify the class when you make the purchase so you need to know what you're buying. In the case of multiple share classes for an equity, I prefer to use the CUSIP, just be consistent and double-check your work.

The CUSIP (Committee on Uniform Security Identification Procedures) is a unique nine-digit alphanumeric code assigned to every tradable security. Every stock, bond, exchange traded fund, mutual fund, hedge fund and closed-end mutual fund have a CUSIP. Before a security can be initially sold in the financial markets it has to have a CUSIP and it will keep that same CUSIP unless it merges with another firm, the bond matures or the fund closes and pays out all funds to shareholders. Bonds always trade by CUSIP due to the detailed nature of the offerings.

Open-end mutual funds have a five-letter symbol that always ends with an X for each class of shares available and a CUSIP number. ETFs and closed-end mutual funds have a symbol determined by which exchange they are traded on and a CUSIP

SOLICITED/UNSOLICITED ORDER

'Solicited/unsolicited' on an order ticket is usually something the average investor will never see. It's more back office brokerage related. Solicited/unsolicited only comes into play when there are two or more people involved in the decision-making process for a transaction. These two boxes (solicited/unsolicited) on a trade ticket are very important and a trade will be rejected if this information is asked for and is missing. Solicited/unsolicited boxes identify the person who initiated the trade.

If your stockbroker calls you up, she has a great idea for you to make some money in a particular stock. If you buy this security at this time, it would be a solicited trade, i.e. your broker solicited you to buy something. If you call up your stockbroker and tell her that you think some stock is going to go through the roof and tell her to buy 100 shares in your investment account, this is an example of an unsolicited trade.

If you have an online trading account, you will always be entering in unsolicited orders. Your trade order is automatically coded that way because there are no salesmen or stockbrokers capable of trading on your behalf.

I like to think of this as "Whose idea was it to make this purchase?" I have had clients talk up a stock and I disagreed with them at that time because I didn't believe that it was a good investment. I don't forget those companies and if in the future I believe that it is now a profitable investment, I will go back to the client and tell them I'm thinking about buying that same company now, are they still interested in owning the security? If they say yes and I buy it for their account, it is a solicited trade because I initialed the conversation about buying that specific security at that time.

EXECUTION PRICE

Execution price has always been one of those weird job-specific terms that bother me. When I started in this business I always wondered who or what was being executed. I decided that for me execution had the meaning of finality or an occurrence that can't be undone, like the execution of a person. Once an event takes place it cannot be undone. For the most part that is true with a security trade. There are circumstances when you can reverse the trade, and we will discuss those in a different section. The execution price is determined at the time the trade takes place.

The execution price is the price paid for a purchase or the price received for the sale of an ownership interest of a security. This price is normally stated in per share price then multiplied by the quantity amount of the trade. It is normal in large orders to have several execution prices. If you are attempting to make a large buy transaction you may 'move the market'. That means that the people on the other side of your transaction don't want to sell that many shares and you have to entice them with a slightly higher price to get the sellers to sell their shares. Each person in the bidding process has their own price. In this case you would buy from the seller with the lowest sale or 'ask' price. When that person's supply is exhausted, you start buying from who has the lowest price now. This cycle will continue on and on all day long until your order has 'filled', the quantity on your order has been reached.

In the case of selling, you would sell to the buyer offering the highest purchase or 'bid' price, then to the seller with the next highest price and so on until your order is filled. The total price received for all shares is divided by the number of shares and that is your price per share minus commissions. For taxes you may be provided with each separate 'tax lot'. A listing of how many shares were purchased at each price level. If this is provided, you can specify which tax lots to sell from and possible reduce taxes implications.

WHAT REALLY HAPPENS WHEN YOU PLACE AN EQUITY ORDER

Most people never know what really happens to their buy or sell orders on Wall Street, but it's pretty simple in most cases. Somewhere your order has to be entered into the electronic system. Once on the electric system there are several places that an order may be routed to match up a buyer to a seller. It first depends on what market controls the trade. If the symbol used to trade that stock has one or two letters in it like 'T' for AT&T or 'NT' for Nortel Networks, it will be traded on the New York Stock Exchange (NYSE). If the trading symbol for a company stock is three letters, it will be traded on either the NYSE or the American Stock Exchange (AMEX). If the trading symbol for a company stock is four letters, it will be traded on the National Association of Security Dealers Automatic Quotation (NASDAQ) system. If the trading symbol has five letters, then it is a mutual fund and goes to either the mutual fund company or a custodial company that holds the mutual fund's securities. Most mutual funds are not held directly with the mutual fund company themselves except for the really big mutual fund companies.

THE NEW YORK STOCK EXCHANGE (NYSE)

If you trade a stock on the New York Stock Exchange (NYSE), chances are that your order will never even make it to the floor of the exchange. That physical location you see on

CNBC is reserved for trade orders over 10,000 shares or more. Most trades are directed to a computer system that matches your order with another party on the other side of the trade. You may be the seller so you are on the 'sell side', and the other party may be the buyer and therefore on the 'buy side' of a trade.

Each stock on the NYSE has a 'specialist', a living and breathing person who will ensure liquidity for that specific security at a designated place on the floor where only that security can be traded whenever the market is open. The price that your trade executes at is determined by the specialist on that particular stock on the floor of the exchange. The specialist gets paid a small part of every transaction of that stock no matter whether the specialist does the deal on the floor or the computer system matches up the buyer and seller. The specialist is the only person allowed to trade in that stock. They are the only person able to see a summary of all pending market and GTC trades. The specialist's goal is to make as many transactions as possible and adjust the price so buyers and sellers get the stock they want at a fair price for both. The specialist may trade several different company securities at that one spot.

The people you see frantically running around the floor of the NYSE have big orders for a stock transaction, they are called 'runners'. They need to get to the specialist before their competitor in the hopes of getting a better price on their order. If five people have big buy orders for IBM, they all rush over to the IBM specialist on the floor. Trading is on a first-come first-served basis. The specialist sees five people arrive in front of them and knows there are orders to fill. The specialist quickly lets the people around him know 'the market' of the security. The market is what the specialist is willing to pay, 'bid price' or just 'bid', or is willing to sell for, 'asking price' or 'ask'. The specialist then needs to know who is buying or selling and the size or quantity. If the specialist can match orders with the people in line, then it's done. Next the specialist takes the remaining orders in sequence of arrival and trades out of their trading account. The specialist has to create a market if none exists so they maintain an open account for themselves where they buy the excess when there are more sellers than buyers. The specialist will sell shares out of their trading account when there are more buyers than sellers.

If bad news on a stock comes out on a company and all the orders in front of the specialist are sell orders, he has to buy all the shares in his own account. But since the specialist controls the price, the law of supply and demand always applies here; at this specific time they will lower the buying price before doing the trades. It also happens in reverse. If everyone in the line is a buyer, then the price goes up. The further back in the line the runner is with their order, the greater the chance of paying a higher price on their trade, so the runners move fast to get the best price for their firm or their firm's clients.

That is also the reason you see prices move during the day. It's the ebb and flow of orders, sometimes leaning to more buyers and sometimes leaning to more sellers. The floor of the NYSE, any exchange in fact, is a nasty cutthroat place. There are examples of unauthorized people barging onto the floor of the NYSE and getting the crap beaten out of them and thrown out. This is an exclusive place and the cost of admission is between $500,000 and 3,000,000 for a 'seat' or the chance to trade down 'on the floor'. Incredibly, it was only recently that women were allowed down there to work.

NASDAQ

The NASDAQ (National Association of Security Dealers Automatic Quotation system) has no physical exchange. It is a computer network connecting buyers and sellers all over the world. I remember when I was working for Dean Witter and training at the World Trade Center. A few of us were invited to the NASDAQ trading area. This place took up half of one floor of the World Trade Center, which means it was a very expansive room.

It was one of the busiest places I had ever been to. There were over one hundred people sitting at their individual desks, and they had at least six compute screens each tracking multiple equities they were responsible for trading in. Several keyboards, mice and a telephone with something like a hundred speed-dial buttons to other traders of the same securities, but these traders were located around the world. There was a multi-rowed conveyor system that delivered paper trade tickets to the traders' desks for them to trade, and once executed these same conveyor systems would return the order ticket for further processing.

These individuals not only traded for the customers of the brokerage firm but also in the brokerage firms trading account. If they saw an opportunity to buy low and sell high, they took it. The profits of these trades went to the brokerage firm. These traders would get a bonus on their trading performance in the brokerage firm's account at the end of the year. This wasn't a place for the old either. It was too pressure-filled and chaotic. Most traders in this room were no older than their lower thirties.

The machines that these traders use show most of the world's trader's bid price and how many shares they are willing to buy at that price, ask price and how many shares they are willing to buy at that price and other trade amount information. The 'bid' is what the traders on any exchange will buy the stock for and how many shares whey will buy at that price. In the case of the NASDAQ, it will be the highest three bidders displayed, so the seller always gets the highest price available. The 'ask' is what the traders are selling the stock for and how many shares at that price they are willing to buy. The three buyers with the lowest 'ask' price are displayed.

AMERICAN STOCK EXCHANGE (AMEX)

The American Stock Exchange (AMEX) has a physical location, close to the New York Stock Exchange, In Lower Manhattan. It is also an electronic exchange with lots of video screens everywhere.

INTERESTING WALL STREET FACT

All of the big brokerage and mutual fund houses have a computer-trading program that kicks in at about two p.m. Have you ever wondered why the market's been up all day long and all of a sudden in the last to hour it goes down? Well, that is the buying and selling power of these computer programs. These huge computer-trading programs are taking into account a vast amount of data backed by billions of dollars of trading assets. The computer-trading programs look at economic data, trading data, they look at the projected inflows and outflows of the mutual funds they manage and will have to adjust for after close of the markets that day. They also look at their individual brokerage firms trading accounts to see if they are too overweighed, too underweighted or overly exposed to what the limits of their market risks are. We are talking about billions of dollars here.

The Security and Exchange Commission has placed rules into effect that if the market moves a certain percentage either up or down, these computer-trading programs have to be shut down and can no longer trade that day. Then it's up to the individual traders to adjust the huge brokerage portfolios to the parameters the computer-trading programs spit out.

Chapter 10

PICKING AND WORKING WITH AN INVESTMENT ADVISOR

The first idea I want to present in this section is how to use your existing professional relationships to keep some checks and balances in your personal finances. The most important person in this picture is you, and you need to remain at the center of your financial universe. One of the professional relationships you can leverage first is your accountant or tax preparer. They get a summary of investments that were bought and sold the previous year for tax purposes, and they should be looking for a few things. If the markets were having a good year and you lost a ton of money in the markets, that's a signal that something is wrong with the way your investments are being managed. It should be your accountant's duty to at least discuss this issue with you.

Another person who should act as a check and balance in your life is your legal advisor. This is another opportunity to discuss any irregularities in your finances. He will handle your will and estate. Are your trust assets in a place where they can be distributed through your will or trust?

Finally there is your insurance agent. He handles your personal insurance needs, maybe your business insurance needs. You need to be knowledgeable in this area also. Know what life insurance **you need**, not what the salesperson wants to sell you. Look at long-term care insurance, it will be very important the older you get. Insurance agents are not the best at investments; they love to sell annuities or loaded mutual funds because they generate huge commissions for them.

Since you already pay these professionals, you may as well use these people for your financial checks and balances. Most of the problems individuals have start when they allow one of these four people to handle or advise on other matters which are not their specialty. The most common situation is that some celebrity lets their agent manage their finances. Later the celebrity finds out they are bankrupt because either the agent had no knowledge of investments and lost a great portion of the celebrity's wealth or the agent stole their money because there were no checks or balances in place. An honest person has no problem having their work challenged by checks and balances.

I have been in the retail side of the business and I know that investment professionals do strike up deals with accountants and lawyers. In exchange for a referral the finance guy will pay the accountant or lawyer part of the revenue the account generates. However, this is illegal, so the deal works that the lawyer calls the investment guy up every quarter. The finance guy tells the lawyer how much an account paid in fees or commissions for the quarter. The percentage is calculated and the lawyer submits a bill to the investment professional for legal services for exactly the amount of his percentage of commissions. Still illegal in my book, but Wall Street is about assets under management and making money. At least in this case, the client has a professional working on their investments. You may want to ask your financial professional if he's paying anyone referral fees for your account.

I was traveling through the Mohave Desert and caught the Motley Fool radio hour on National Public Radio. One of the callers had recently come into a large inheritance and was asking what attributes they should look for when looking to hire an investment advisor. Their advice was to interview at least four advisors, and ask the prospective advisor how they got paid. They also said to avoid any advisor that recommended only one family of funds, especially if the funds are branded to the company that they are working for. I thought that this was a good start to the answer.

I did a search on Goggle using 'how to pick a financial planner' or 'selecting a financial planner' and got back some very good sites. Read a few of the articles, it will be very empowering. You could spend almost as much time and energy selecting who will manage and provide you with financial advice as the actual selection of your asset allocation and investments. It will be time well spent. Don't just use the person your parents or your brother or sister uses, but you can listen to why they chose that particular person. This should be a long-term relationship, do your homework. And if by chance you pick someone and they don't satisfy your needs, look again for that right person.

You will need to meet several investment professionals. This should be a multi-meeting process to determine who will handle your finances. The first meeting should be centered on the services that each planner offers. You can and should learn a lot from this process. You should be told by the advisor what their personal type of investing style is, if the advisor will help with your current employer retirement plans, and if they advise on or help with your other investment needs like home or car financing ideas. Stockbrokers and salespeople are very skilled at not directly answering your questions; make sure your questions are answered directly.

You must be able to communicate with your financial advisor. This is a very intimate relationship and you will need to be comfortable discussing many uncomfortable subjects with them. Look for open, intelligent conversation free from industry specific jargon and look for terminology that you understand. If the person you are interviewing gets angry and won't give you the information you ask for, then they are not the one for you.

After sex, personal financial matters are the most difficult topics to discuss with people. I tell my male clients that our relationship will be the most intimate relationship they will ever have. They will eventually trust me enough to tell me things they would tell no other. I tell my female clients that after their gynecologist, I will be the second most intimate relationship they will ever have. This requires a lot of trust on their side, which I will earn. I also look them in the eye and tell them I am a 'keeper of secrets'. Which means to me that any sensitive subjects we discuss are never spoken about again unless they bring up the subject.

Watch for designations after their name: CFA (Chartered Financial Analyst), CFP (Chartered Financial Planner), and ChFC (Chartered Financial Consultant). This shows that the salesperson has studied a wide body of investment topics and passed a difficult test or tests to prove their knowledge. These are designations you have to earn, and they show commitment to their clients and the industry.

The questions listed here should be asked of anyone handling your financial matters:

- What is your college degree in?

- Any memberships or designations that show your continued financial education?

- How long have you been in the financial planning business?

- Have you had any arbitration or litigation actions taken

against you?

- How do you get paid?

- What type of investing style do you use and explain it to me?

- Do you provide reports that tell me the performance of my accounts?

- Do you provide long and short-term capital gains reports for tax purposes?

- Will you help with my current employer retirement plan?

- What other services can you offer me?

- Will you provide me with some references?

- Who will **ACTUALLY** be handling the trading decisions in MY account?

- Where will my accounts be custodied?

Questions that they should ask are:

- How much have you saved?

- How much do you make?

- Are there any predictable large cash flows in the future? College for your kids, down payment for house, bonus from work etc.?

- When do you want to retire?

You should have prepared copies of all of your investment and retirement accounts for this person to review. They can't help you to their fullest if you withhold any important information.

There are many ways to check up on your prospective financial planner. Ask for a copy of their U-4. This lists the licenses they have with the SEC and any problems they may have faced by regulators. You can also go to the Securities and Exchange Commission website www.sec.gov for more information about your financial advisor, all you will need is their name and the company they work for. They also have a section of helpful advice on picking a financial advisor.

The second meeting should be more investment focused. You should be presented with an investment plan. That plan should consist of a recommended asset allocation specifically designed for you and what specific investments will be used. It should also include how the asset allocation will change over time and adjust for varying market conditions. An Investment Policy Statement should be presented to list all of the individual's accounts and the investment goals, types of investments that can be used and benchmarks used for evaluating the performance of the portfolio. The Investment Policy Statement isn't a requirement but it is a helpful tool when investing and comparing performance. It should include information on where your accounts will be transferred to and what company will 'custody' or hold your assets. It will tell you if you will have online viewing capability so you can monitor your investments. A sample statement should be included so that you can see how what information you will be receiving and how it is organized. It is very important to have a detailed meeting going over your specific account statement when your accounts are transferred in to the new accounts.

DIFFERENT TYPES OF INVESTMENT COMPANIES

REGISTERED INVESTMENT ADVISORS

Registered Investment Advisors (RIA or IA's) have to disclose to you all kinds of information that mutual fund companies, insurance salespeople, or stockbrokers don't have to. Information like: any conflict of interests that may exist in servicing your account, personal education, financial experience, employment history, how we charge our clients, what types of investment we use and many other items. This information is listed on our ADV forms, which we have to update yearly and submit to the Securities and Exchange Commission. We also agree and sign a contract on how and when you will pay the RIA firm. This is normally either a percentage of assets under management or a flat fee is the most common. The fee will be deducted from your account, usually quarterly.

Registered Investment Advisors (RIA) usually custody their accounts at a larger brokerage firm. The larger firm does all of the account maintenance, custody of assets, account reporting and execution of the trades. The custody firm is paid by charging a commission on all of the trades, but the RIA doesn't or shouldn't receive any of the commissions because they are paid by the contract negotiated between you and them. By only having a custodial relationship with the larger firm the RIA doesn't have any obligation to any company or product line. RIA's are supposed to be completely independent.

RIA's may also have a minimum, I did, $100,000 of investable assets was my minimum. I'm a generalist who handled a wide variety of accounts. I managed stock-only accounts, bond-only accounts, and accounts with a mix of stocks and bonds. Most RIA firms specialize in one or two types of specialized investing; an example would be asset allocation, equity only or bonds only.

BROKERAGE FIRMS

There are several types of firms offering investment advice. You will recognize the large Wall Street firms like Morgan Stanley, Merrill Lynch and others like that. After all of the scandals they have been a part of and with my personal experience I really couldn't recommend this type of firm. The stockbrokers who are supposed to be working for you actually work for the Wall Street firm first, then for themselves, and finally for you. Every week I read about another large firm breaking the law or paying a big fine. Do you really want this type of firm managing your money? On the positive side they do have a vast array of services they can offer such as trust or estate planning. If you have a good-sized portfolio – over two million – then you may want to talk to one of these larger firms.

INDEPENDENT ADVISORS

This group of financial professionals can offer a wide variety of services. They may or may not have ties to a large firm. Ask. These professionals are normally series 7 licensed so they can sell stocks, individual bonds, mutual funds, the services of RIAs and brokerage firms. If they are Series 6 licensed, then they can only sell mutual funds. If they have a Series 63, they can sell products in all 50 states. If they have an insurance license, they can sell insurance products like life or health insurance or annuities. They can also sell products that pay them by an internal fee.

INSURANCE AGENTS

Insurance agents usually have a Series 6 security license. They can sell mutual funds and annuities. Insurance agents, like stockbrokers, work first for their companies, then for themselves, and finally for you. These insurance salespeople usually do not have the training or resources available to them that most other financial planners have. They love to sell annuity products because they make a very big upfront commission, 5% to 16%. With annuities you normally get stuck with higher internal expenses than a mutual fund, and bigger penalties if you cash out of these products before the surrender period ends, which can last up to 16 years. Annuities are retirement vehicles, so if you take out money before you reach retirement age, even more penalties could apply. There are too many good investment products out there that have no surrender charges that you can use in place of annuities.

On the plus side, annuities, because they are an insurance product, are usually litigation proof. This is how doctors and celebrities can shelter money from creditors or lawsuits.

ON-LINE BROKERAGE ACCOUNTS

If you want a little more variety than just mutual funds and still want to do it yourself, you can open up an online brokerage account. You should look at services that are available and the commissions you will pay for all of the different types of investments you may be buying. The services vary widely from one company to another so educate yourself first. There are several comparisons done on these Internet brokerage firms, and I would strongly recommend you read them before picking a firm to do business with. Also make sure your accounts are insured against theft or if the firm goes bankrupt. No one will insure against investment loses, just thought I'd mention that. The online brokerage firms have to follow most of the regular investment legislation so as long as you go with a known name you should be all right.

A FEW FINAL THOUGHTS

Investing your personal wealth is very intimidating. It doesn't help that most of the people in the investment community use lots of jargon when communicating. I know that part of this is to cover up their own investment knowledge shortcomings, but mainly it's to keep you stupid and dependant on them to make your investment decisions. If you understand half of what you have read in this book, you probably know more practical investment knowledge than most investment salespeople. Find someone who will partner with you to make sound investment decisions to benefit you, and not their paycheck.

If this is your first investment book, don't make it your last. I plan on being a student of investing and the concepts of investing for the rest of my life. That philosophy goes for all knowledge areas of my life. I hope you will join me! It doesn't matter what you study or learn about, just keep on learning.

I stated at the beginning of this book, "I'm passionate about investing." I absolutely love what I do for a living and can't see myself doing anything else as a profession. Some of the other passions in my life are opera, travel – both domestic and international, anything that involves danger and risk (but not heights), and learning the origins of words and phrases. The passions in my life have changed or morphed over time. I never thought that I would ever stop racing cars. The thrills, danger and emotional highs were better than any recreation drug I took in the past. My body has a weird way of telling me to stop activities and I became very sensitive to the g-forces experienced when racing to the point of getting carsick, so it was time to stop that activity.

The point that I'm trying to get across is to find something that you are passionate about. Explore these passions and enjoy the experience. If you don't have any passions, then travel someplace very different than you're used to, explore a park, learn to scuba dive, ride a horse, learn to fly a plane, shoot a bow and arrow, climb a mountain, or any other activity that isn't within your comfort zone. If you physically can't do these types of activities, buy a book on the subject and read about it. I read the book *Into Thin Air*, which is about an attempt to climb Mount Everest. I was really thinking about doing something like this, but after reading the book I knew that this activity wasn't for me. I really enjoyed the book and how it was written, however.

The next book I may write is about all the wild adventures while I was in the Marine Corps, working as a whitewater river guide and ocean lifeguard, and when I raced cars. I still enjoy wild times, crazy activities and adventurous travel so I may have some other adventures to talk about.

I want to thank you for reading my book. I genuinely hope that you have learned and understood some helpful information. Don't be afraid to put what you have learned into practice. Remember to invest in moderation. Don't take any huge changes unless you have thought through the changes and discussed them with someone else.

Scott

1905273

Made in the USA